METAL PROJECTS

BOOK 1

By
John R. Walker
Bel Air High School
Bel Air, Md.

South Holland, Illinois
THE GOODHEART-WILLCOX CO., Inc.
Publishers

INTRODUCTION

Many instructors of metalworking are on the lookout for worthwhile projects that make use of a variety of manufacturing and fabricating techniques. They want projects for students with a wide range of abilities...projects that will challenge their students. It is for these purposes that this book is especially intended.

Projects are presented for these metalworking areas:

Sheet Metal	Foundry
Machine Shop	Art Metal
Bench Metal	Welding and Forging

You will note that tolerances, procedures and bills of material have been omitted. On some drawings, only basic dimensions are given; on some only project suggestions are presented.

Tolerances have been omitted so the instructor may establish his own standards. These are not necessarily the same for intermediate students, as for beginners. Material lists and procedures were omitted to encourage the student to do his own planning and organizing.

The projects in this book are of proven student interest. They will provide attractive and useful take home items. And, they will lend considerable prestige to your shop, if they are first prominently displayed for a period of time in the shop area.

John R. Walker

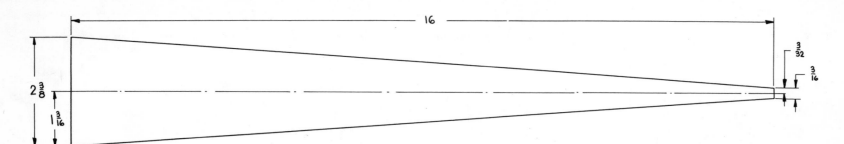

BODY
2 REQ'D

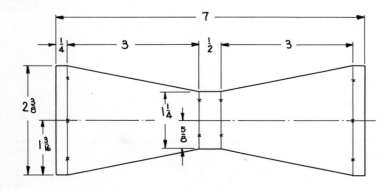

BASE

MADE FROM $\frac{7}{8}$ D. COPPER TUBING
CLOSE BASE AND FLARE LIP.

CANDLE HOLDER

FOLK ART TYPE CANDLESTICK

1. Material: 16 ga. brass (half-hard) or 16 ga.
   black iron sheet.

2. Finish: Polished (brass) or painted flat black.
   Trim as desired.

3. Cut pieces to shape, remove burrs, shape over
   full size pattern and solder or braze together.

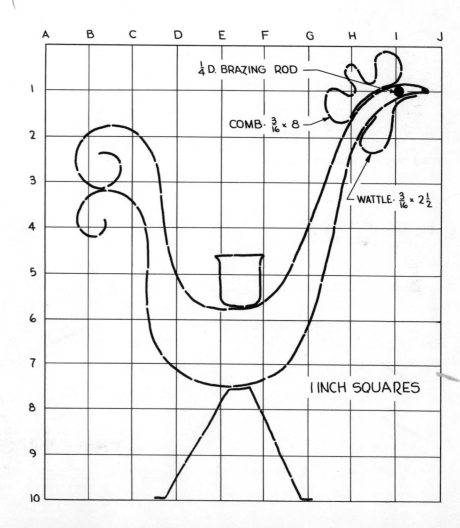

$\frac{1}{4}$ D. BRAZING ROD

COMB - $\frac{3}{16} \times 8$

WATTLE - $\frac{3}{16} \times 2\frac{1}{2}$

1 INCH SQUARES

5

SERVING TRAY

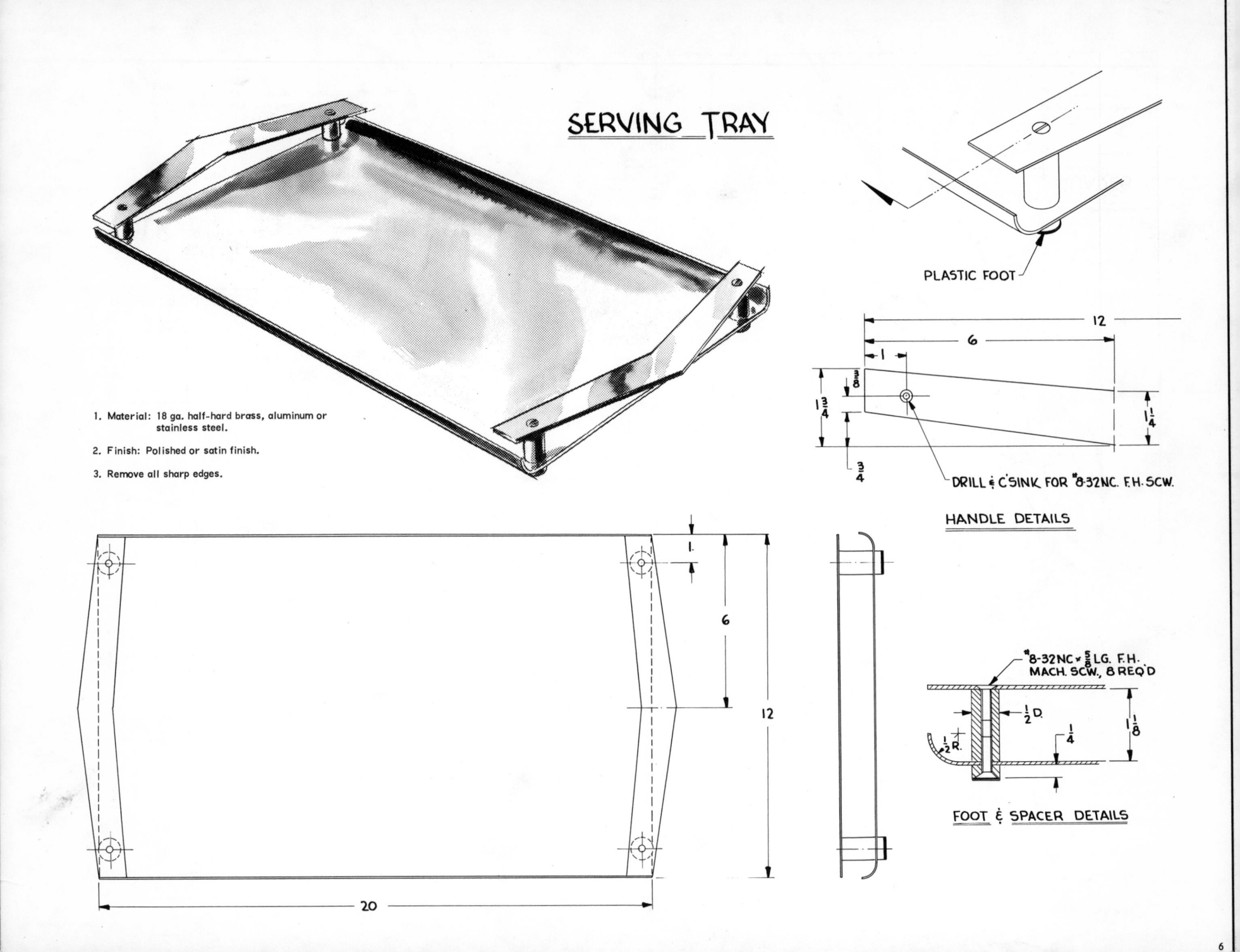

1. Material: 18 ga. half-hard brass, aluminum or stainless steel.

2. Finish: Polished or satin finish.

3. Remove all sharp edges.

PLASTIC FOOT

12

6

1

$1\frac{3}{4}$

$\frac{3}{8}$

$\frac{3}{4}$

$1\frac{1}{4}$

DRILL & C'SINK FOR #8-32NC. F.H. SCW.

HANDLE DETAILS

1

6

12

20

#8-32NC × $\frac{5}{8}$ LG. F.H. MACH. SCW., 8 REQ'D

$\frac{1}{2}$ D.

$\frac{1}{2}$ R.

$\frac{1}{4}$

$1\frac{1}{8}$

FOOT & SPACER DETAILS

TOOLMAKER'S VISE

1. Material: Cold finished steel.

2. Finish: Machine all over. Finish grind if a surface grinder is available.

3. A straight knurl may be substituted for the diamond knurl indicated.

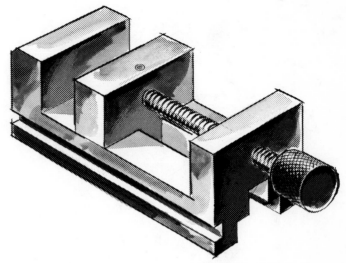

BODY

JAW

8-32NC × 3/8 LG. FULL DOG PT.

SCREW

1/16 D. × 1/2 LG. PIN AT ASSEMBLY

GUIDE

#8-32NC × 1/2 LG. F.H. MACH. SCW.

TOLERANCES UNLESS NOTED
FRACTIONS ± 1/64
DECIMALS ± .003
ANGULAR ± 1°

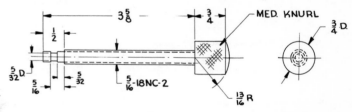

SCREW

MED. KNURL
3/4 D.
3/4
3 5/8
1/2
5/32 D.
5/16
5/32
5/16-18NC-2
13/16 R

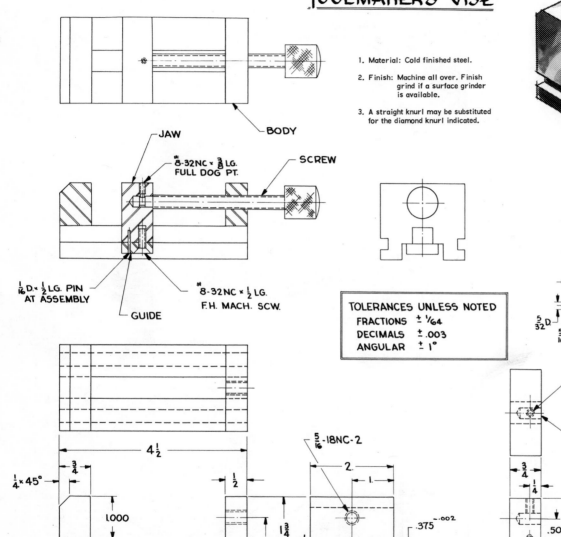

4 1/2
3/4
1/4 × 45°
1.000
1 5/16
1 3/4
1/2
5/16-18NC-2
2.
1.
.375 −.002
1/4
3/16
.500
.500
1.000
.250

BODY

#8-32NC-2
1/4 D. × 1/2 DP.
3/4
1/4
1/4
.500
1 3/8
2
1
#8-32NC-2
.375 +.002
.250
.500

JAW

3/16 D. C'SINK 82° × 5/16 D.
3/4
3/4
1/4
1/8
1/4
1/16 D. AT ASSEMBLY

GUIDE

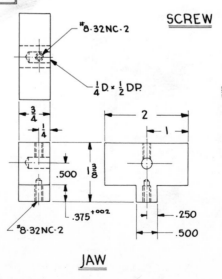
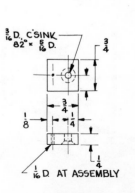

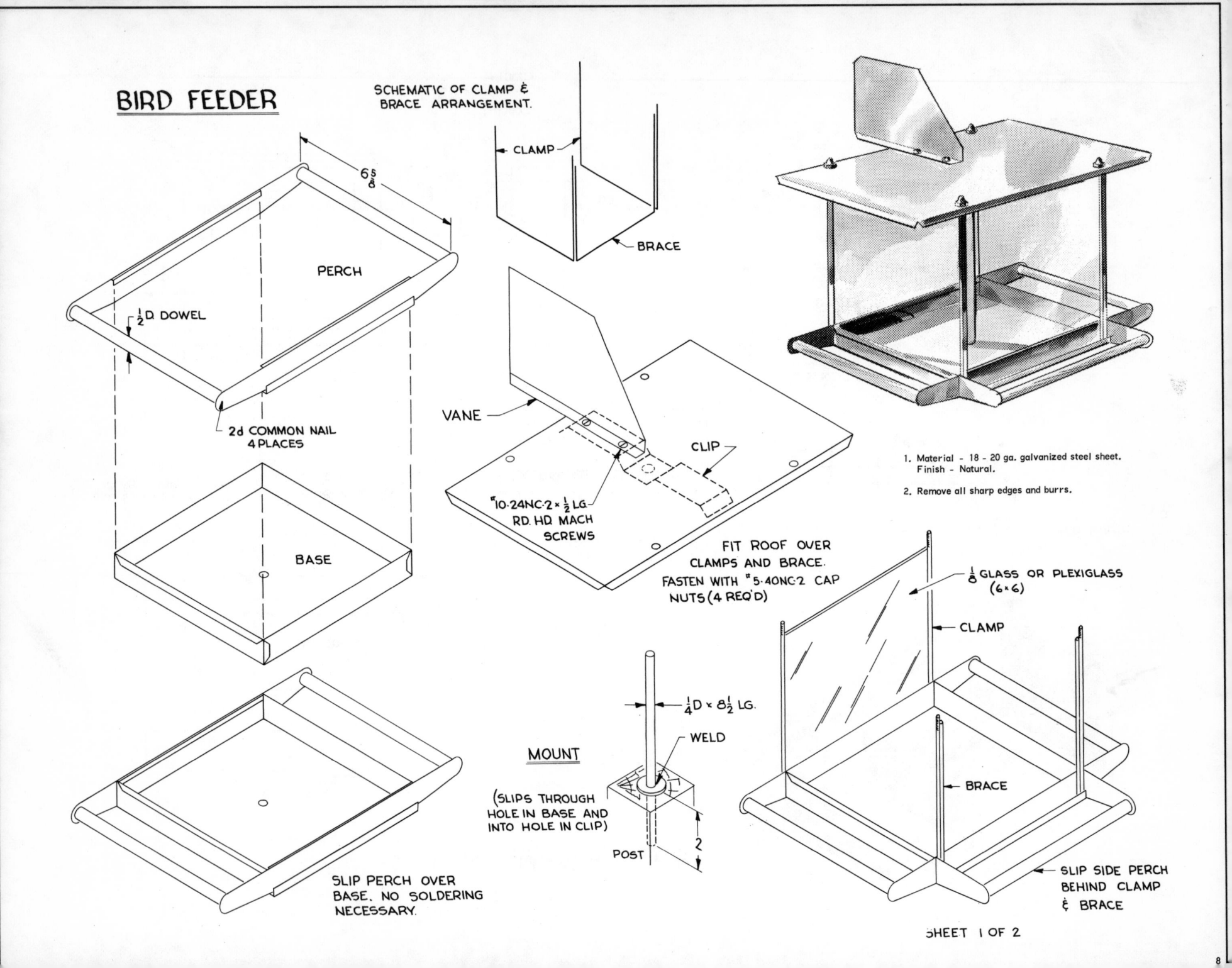

BIRD FEEDER

SCHEMATIC OF CLAMP &
BRACE ARRANGEMENT.

CLAMP

BRACE

$6\frac{5}{8}$

PERCH

$\frac{1}{2}$ D DOWEL

2d COMMON NAIL
4 PLACES

BASE

VANE

CLIP

#10-24NC-2 × $\frac{1}{2}$ LG.
RD. HD. MACH
SCREWS

FIT ROOF OVER
CLAMPS AND BRACE.
FASTEN WITH #5-40NC-2 CAP
NUTS (4 REQ'D)

1. Material - 18 - 20 ga. galvanized steel sheet.
   Finish - Natural.

2. Remove all sharp edges and burrs.

$\frac{1}{8}$ GLASS OR PLEXIGLASS
(6×6)

CLAMP

$\frac{1}{4}$ D × $8\frac{1}{2}$ LG.

WELD

MOUNT

(SLIPS THROUGH
HOLE IN BASE AND
INTO HOLE IN CLIP)

POST

2

BRACE

SLIP PERCH OVER
BASE. NO SOLDERING
NECESSARY.

SLIP SIDE PERCH
BEHIND CLAMP
& BRACE

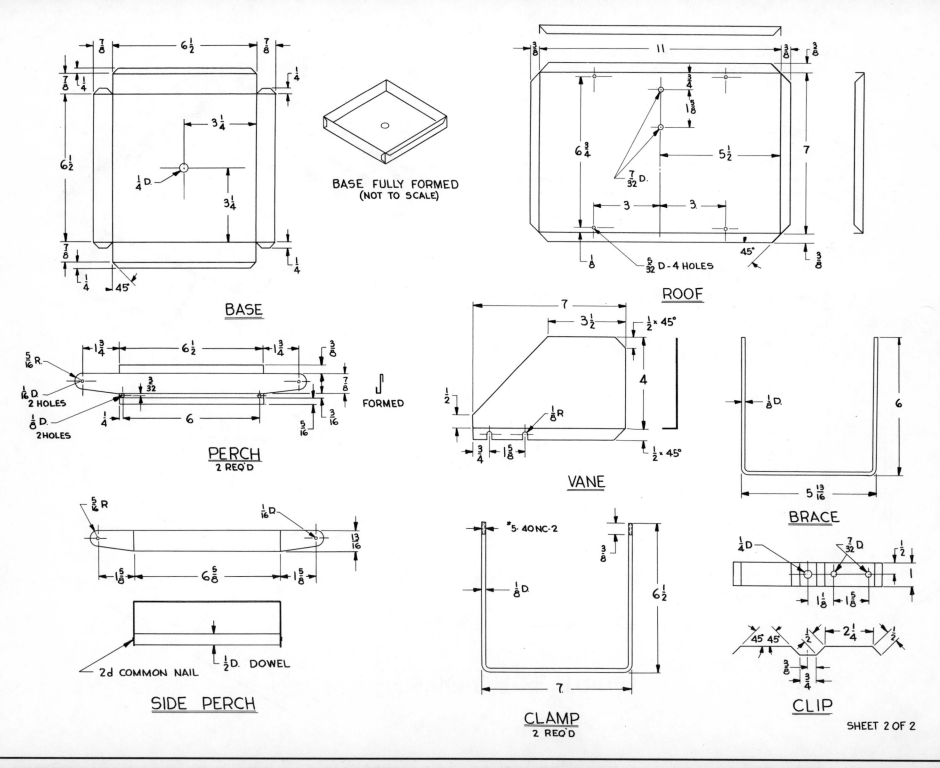

BASE

BASE FULLY FORMED
(NOT TO SCALE)

ROOF

PERCH
2 REQ'D

VANE

BRACE

SIDE PERCH

CLAMP
2 REQ'D

CLIP

SINGLE TILE TRIVET

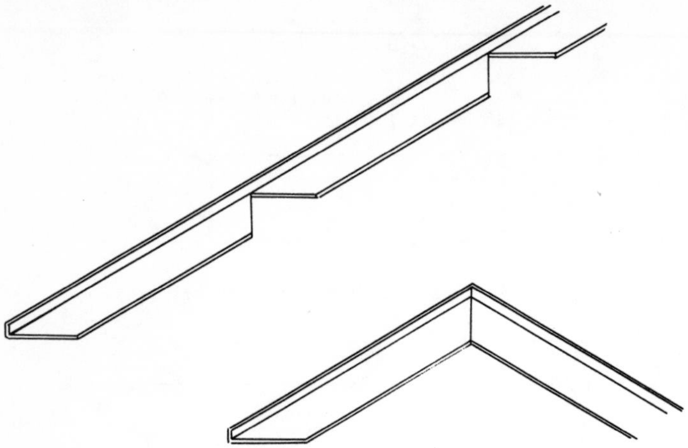

1. Material: Body - 16 or 18 ga. half-hard brass
   or black annealed steel sheet.
   Handles - 1/8 dia. brazing rod.

2. Finish: Polished or painted flat black.

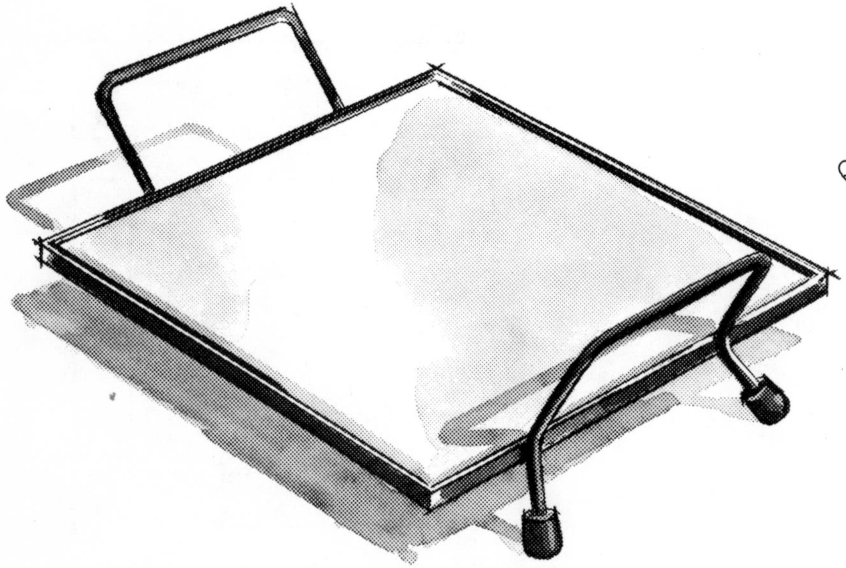

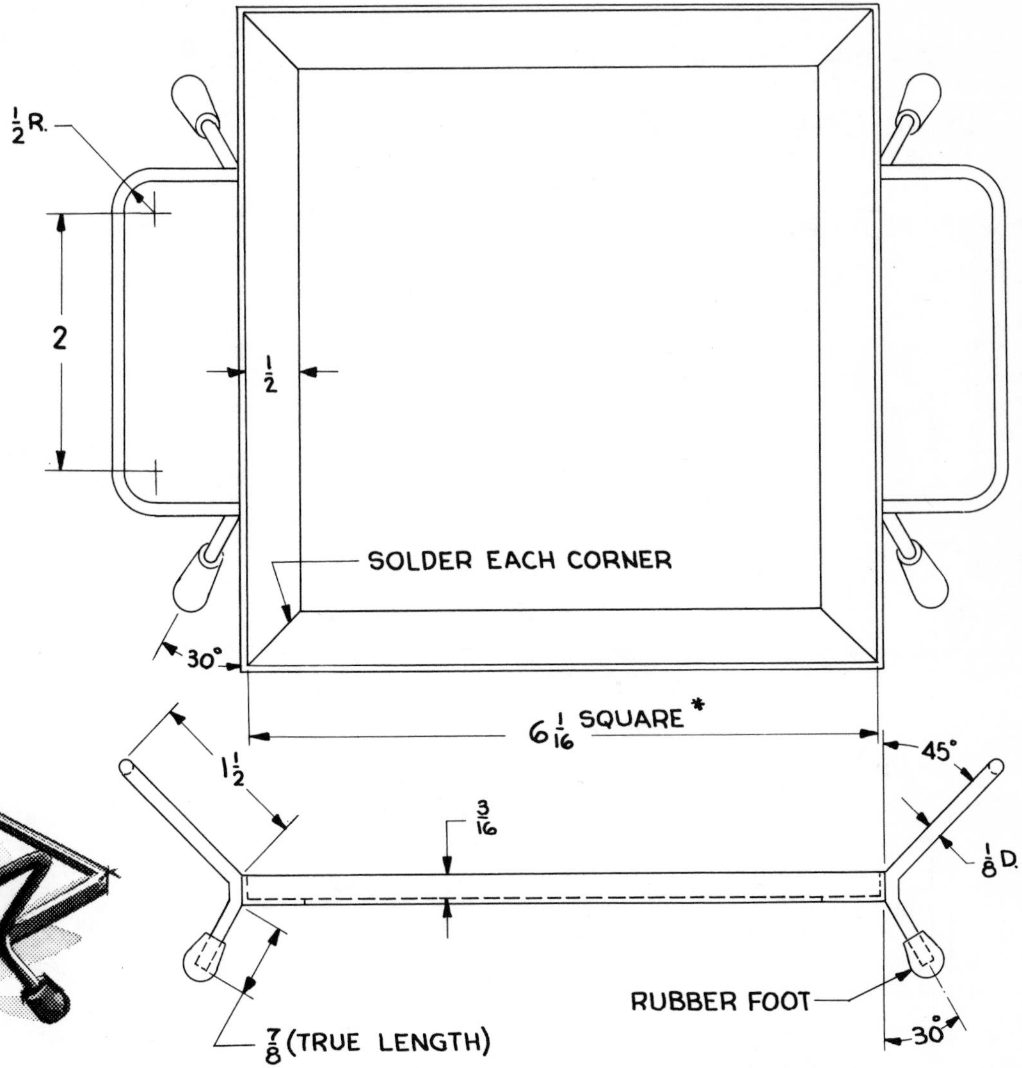

$\frac{1}{2}$ R.

2

$\frac{1}{2}$

SOLDER EACH CORNER

30°

$6\frac{1}{16}$ SQUARE *

$1\frac{1}{2}$

$\frac{3}{16}$

45°

$\frac{1}{8}$ D.

RUBBER FOOT

30°

$\frac{7}{8}$ (TRUE LENGTH)

*TILE DIMENSIONS VARY SLIGHTLY. CHECK
TILE TO BE USED FOR EXACT DIMENSIONS.

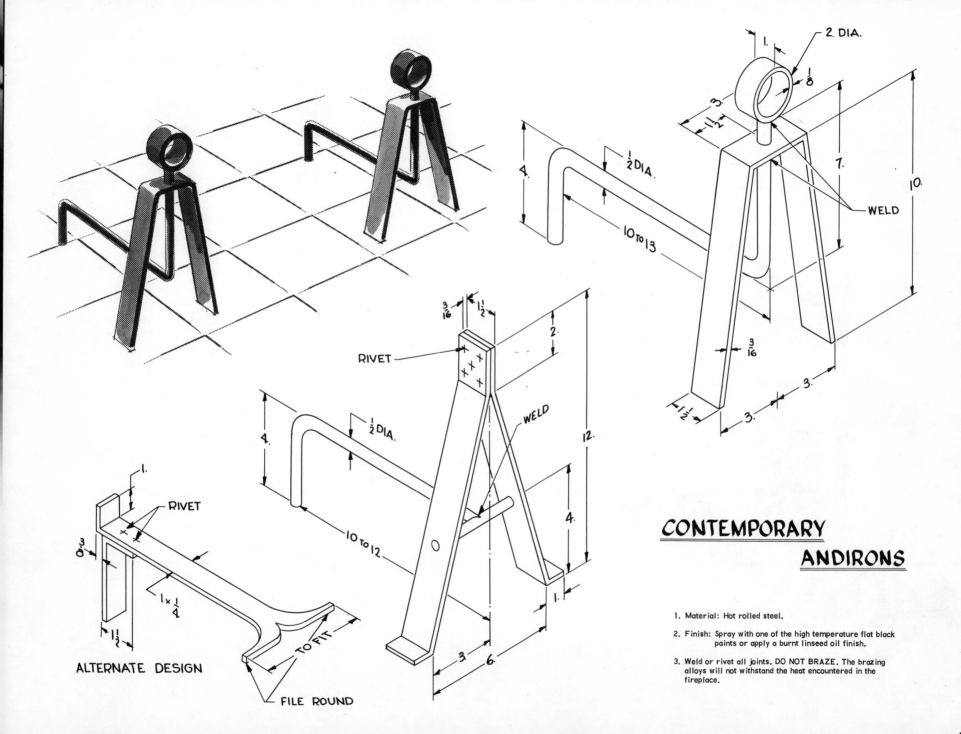

CONTEMPORARY ANDIRONS

ALTERNATE DESIGN

RIVET

FILE ROUND

TO FIT

$1 \times \frac{1}{4}$

RIVET

WELD

$\frac{1}{2}$ DIA.

10 to 12

$\frac{3}{16}$

$1\frac{1}{2}$

$\frac{1}{2}$ DIA.

10 to 13

WELD

2. DIA.

$\frac{1}{8}$

3.

$1\frac{1}{2}$

7.

10.

$\frac{3}{16}$

1. Material: Hot rolled steel.

2. Finish: Spray with one of the high temperature flat black paints or apply a burnt linseed oil finish.

3. Weld or rivet all joints. DO NOT BRAZE. The brazing alloys will not withstand the heat encountered in the fireplace.

BUFFING HEAD

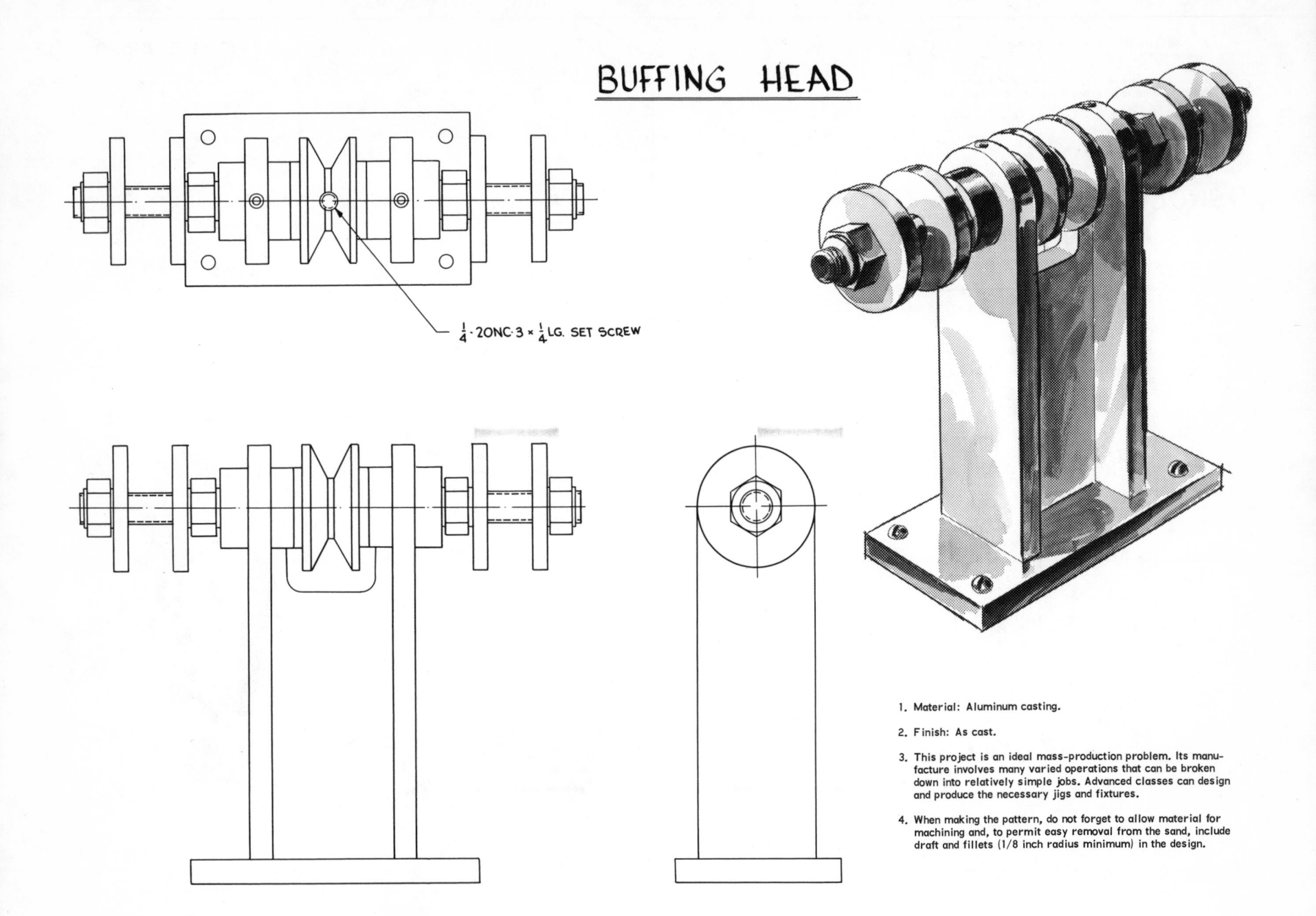

$\frac{1}{4}$-20NC-3 × $\frac{1}{4}$ LG. SET SCREW

1. Material: Aluminum casting.

2. Finish: As cast.

3. This project is an ideal mass-production problem. Its manufacture involves many varied operations that can be broken
   down into relatively simple jobs. Advanced classes can design
   and produce the necessary jigs and fixtures.

4. When making the pattern, do not forget to allow material for
   machining and, to permit easy removal from the sand, include
   draft and fillets (1/8 inch radius minimum) in the design.

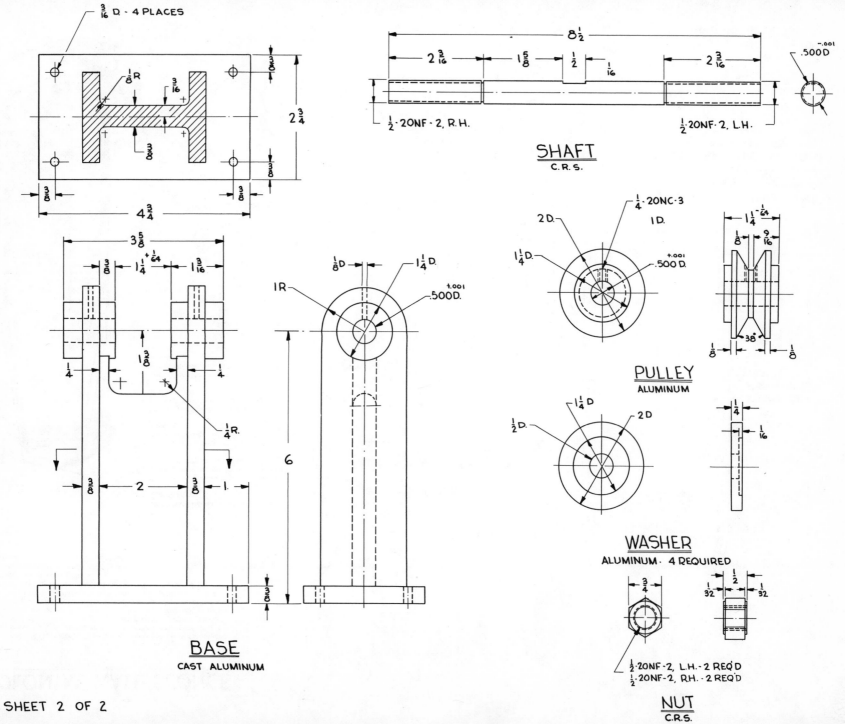

$\frac{3}{16}$ D. - 4 PLACES

$\frac{1}{8}$ R

$\frac{3}{16}$

$2\frac{3}{4}$

$4\frac{3}{4}$

$\frac{3}{8}$

BASE
CAST ALUMINUM

$3\frac{5}{8}$

$1\frac{1}{4}^{+\frac{1}{64}}$

$1\frac{3}{16}$

$\frac{3}{8}$

$1\frac{3}{8}$

$\frac{1}{4}$

$\frac{1}{4}$ R.

$\frac{1}{8}$ D.

$1\frac{1}{4}$ D.

1 R

.500 D.

6

$\frac{3}{8}$

2

$\frac{3}{8}$

1

$\frac{3}{8}$

$8\frac{1}{2}$

$2\frac{3}{16}$

$1\frac{5}{8}$

$\frac{1}{2}$

$\frac{1}{16}$

$2\frac{3}{16}$

.500D

$\frac{1}{2}$·20NF·2, R.H.

$\frac{1}{2}$·20NF·2, L.H.

SHAFT
C.R.S.

$\frac{1}{4}$·20NC·3

2 D.

1 D.

$1\frac{1}{4}$ D.

.500 D.

$1\frac{1}{4}^{-\frac{1}{64}}$

$\frac{1}{8}$

$\frac{9}{16}$

38°

$\frac{1}{8}$

$\frac{1}{8}$

PULLEY
ALUMINUM

$1\frac{1}{4}$ D

$\frac{1}{2}$ D.

2 D

$\frac{1}{4}$

$\frac{1}{16}$

WASHER
ALUMINUM · 4 REQUIRED

$\frac{3}{4}$

$\frac{1}{32}$

$\frac{1}{2}$

$\frac{1}{32}$

$\frac{1}{2}$·20NF·2, L.H.· 2 REQ'D
$\frac{1}{2}$·20NF·2, R.H.· 2 REQ'D

NUT
C.R.S.

COLONIAL WALL SCONCE

Sconces were made in a myriad of shapes and sizes during colonial times. The one illustrated was one of the simpler designs. It was made of tinplate (although one sample was of copper) and could be found in the home of a tradesman. Its sole purpose was to reflect as much of the feeble candlelight as possible and to protect the wall or cabinet from the flame. As furniture of the colonial period is again in popular demand, the sconce has many practical and ornamental uses in today's home.

1. Material: Tinplate - XX thickness (0.0175 in.).

2. Be careful of sharp edges and burrs common to sheet metal work. Get cuts and soldering burns treated promptly.

3. Develop a full size paper pattern and check for size and fit before cutting metal.

4. Use sharp tools and a soldering copper that is hot enough and properly tinned.

5. Wash down the project with warm soapy water after soldering to remove flux and dirt.

EDGES & TABS FORMED

BASE

CANDLE HOLDER

FLARE LIP SLIGHTLY

SOLDER

REFLECTOR

ALLOWANCE FOR DOUBLE HEM

TOP

FOLDS MADE

ALLOWANCE FOR DOUBLE HEM

FRONT

FRONT   CANDLE HOLDER

SET BASE TABS INTO HEM OF FRONT AND SOLDER

SWEAT SOLDER CANDLE HOLDER TO BASE

SET BACK EDGE OF BASE INTO BOTTOM HEM OF REFLECTOR

SOLDER WING TABS OF FRONT TO REFLECTOR

PAPER PUNCH

PROBLEM: Use three of these units and develop an adjustable punch that can be used to correctly space and punch the holes in a paper sheet so that it will fit the standard notebook.

#7 DRILL $\frac{5}{8}$ DP.
$\frac{1}{4}$-20NC × $\frac{1}{2}$ DP. 2 HOLES

$\frac{15}{64}$ DRILL -.250 $^{+.001}$ REAM AT ASSEMBLY

$\frac{1}{4}$

$\frac{1}{2}$

$\frac{1}{4}$

2.

$\frac{3}{4}$ R.

$\frac{3}{4}$ D.

$\frac{1}{2}$

$\frac{1}{2}$

$1\frac{1}{8}$

$2\frac{1}{4}$

$\frac{1}{8}$

$\frac{5}{16}$ $\frac{13}{16}$ $\frac{5}{8}$

BODY
ALUMINUM

PRESS FIT

$\frac{1}{16}$ D × $\frac{3}{8}$ LG. PIN

WASHER

$\frac{1}{2}$

$\frac{5}{16}$ $\frac{13}{16}$ $\frac{1}{4}$ (REF.)

2. SQ.

"F" DRILL, C'SINK 82° × $\frac{1}{2}$ D. 2 HOLES

$\frac{5}{16}$ D. C'BORE × $\frac{1}{4}$ DP.

1

BASE
ALUMINUM

-.001
.249 D.

KNURL

$\frac{3}{8}$

$\frac{1}{16}$ D.

$2\frac{7}{8}$

$1\frac{1}{2}$

5°

PLUNGER
DRILL ROD

$\frac{1}{4}$ I.D.

$1\frac{1}{8}$

10 TURNS

SPRING
.045 D. MUSIC WIRE

$\frac{7}{8}$ R

$\frac{1}{16}$

$\frac{13}{16}$

$\frac{3}{8}$

$1\frac{1}{4}$

$\frac{1}{2}$

$\frac{1}{4}$ D. × $\frac{3}{8}$ DP.

HEAD
ALUMINUM

$\frac{1}{2}$ $\frac{1}{4}$

$\frac{3}{64}$

WASHER
C.R.S.

15

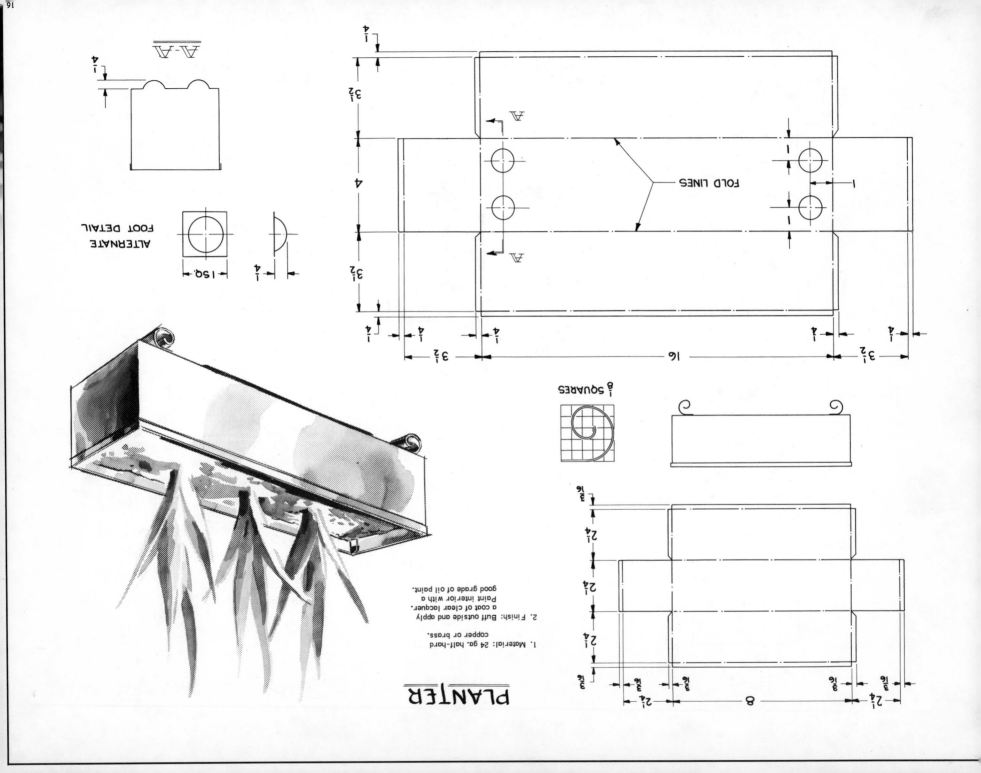

A-A

ALTERNATE FOOT DETAIL

1 SQ.

FOLD LINES

⅛ SQUARES

PLANTER

1. Material: 24 ga. half-hard copper or brass.

2. Finish: Buff outside and apply a coat of clear lacquer. Paint interior with a good grade of oil paint.

PATIO TABLE

SEE DETAIL "A"

$12\frac{1}{4}$ $12\frac{1}{4}$

1. Material: Top - 18 ga. annealed steel sheet.
   Legs - 1/8 x 1/2 band iron.

2. Finish: Paint color (white or flat black) will be
   determined by the tile colors.

3. Remove all sharp edges before painting. Four
   6-inch tiles are specified. However, they may
   vary in size and the actual top dimensions will
   be governed by the tiles that will be used.

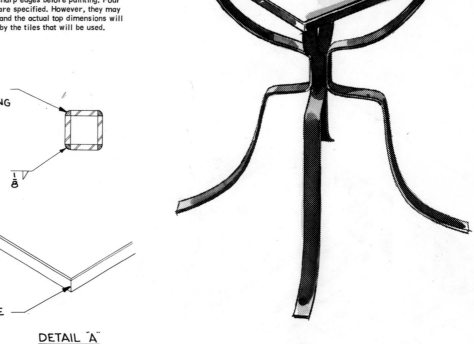

SMOOTH IN
AFTER WELDING

$\frac{1}{8}$

$\frac{1}{4}$

SEE DETAIL "B"

18

$1\frac{1}{2}$ SQUARES

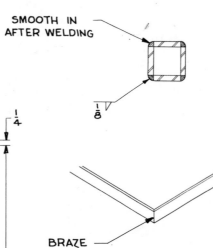

BRAZE

DETAIL "A"

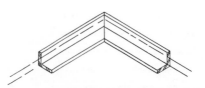

ALTERNATE TOP DETAILS
$\frac{1}{4}$ PLATE GLASS SET IN $\frac{1}{2} \times \frac{1}{2} \times \frac{1}{8}$ ∠

DETAIL "B"

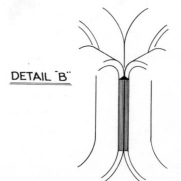

MACHINE WORK TABLE

CLAMP SCREW

$\frac{1}{4}$-20NC-3 × $\frac{1}{4}$ LG. SKT HD.
SET SCREW-FULL DOG POINT

GUIDE PIN
2 REQ'D

SOLID BODY

CLAMP BODY

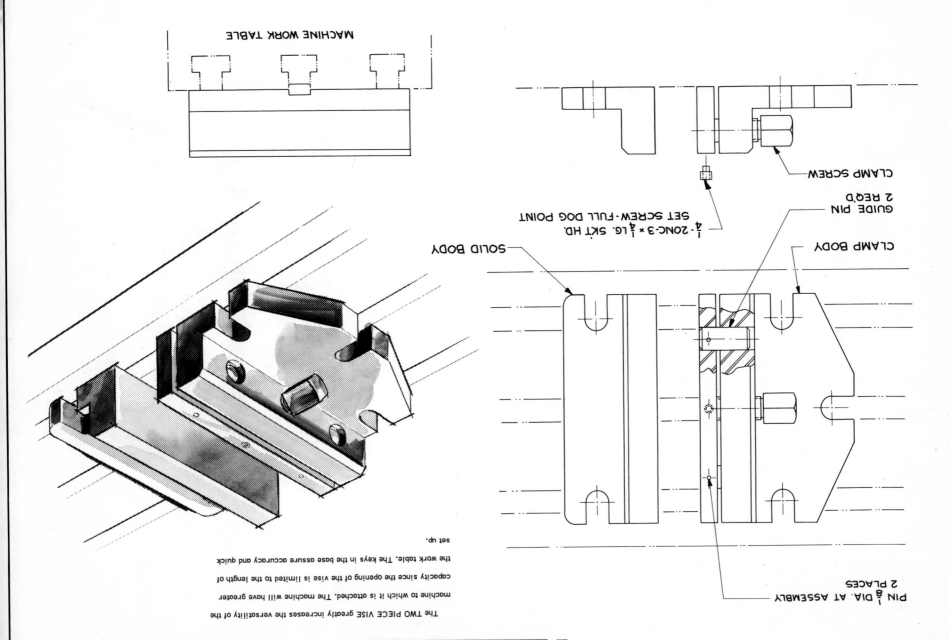

PIN $\frac{1}{8}$ DIA. AT ASSEMBLY
2 PLACES

The TWO PIECE VISE greatly increases the versatility of the
machine to which it is attached. The machine will have greater
capacity since the opening of the vise is limited to the length of
the work table. The keys in the base assure accuracy and quick
set up.

TWO PIECE VISE

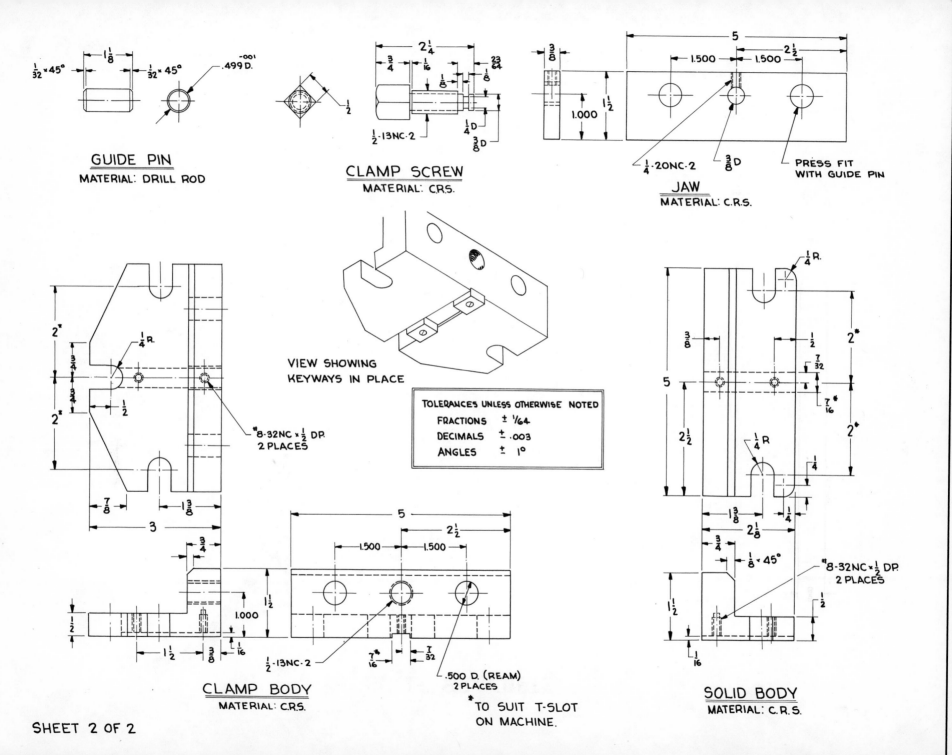

GUIDE PIN
MATERIAL: DRILL ROD

CLAMP SCREW
MATERIAL: C.R.S.

JAW
MATERIAL: C.R.S.

$\frac{1}{4}$-20NC-2

$\frac{3}{8}$D

PRESS FIT WITH GUIDE PIN

VIEW SHOWING
KEYWAYS IN PLACE

TOLERANCES UNLESS OTHERWISE NOTED

FRACTIONS ± $\frac{1}{64}$
DECIMALS ± .003
ANGLES ± 1°

#8-32NC x $\frac{1}{2}$ DP.
2 PLACES

CLAMP BODY
MATERIAL: C.R.S.

.500 D. (REAM)
2 PLACES

* TO SUIT T-SLOT ON MACHINE.

SOLID BODY
MATERIAL: C.R.S.

#8-32NC x $\frac{1}{2}$ DP.
2 PLACES

SHELF BRACKETS

DESIGN PROBLEM: DEVELOP A METHOD THAT WILL HOLD THE BRACKET SOLIDLY TO THE WALL YET PERMIT IT TO BE MOVED EASILY.

1 SQUARES

¾ SQUARES

¾ SQUARES

1. Material:
   Shelf bracket — band iron (sizes noted on plans).
   Shelf — 3/8, 1/2 or 3/4 wood depending upon bracket size.

2. Finish: Shelf bracket — Paint flat black.
   Wood shelf — finish natural.

3. Shelf may be set in place or attached to bracket with wood screws.

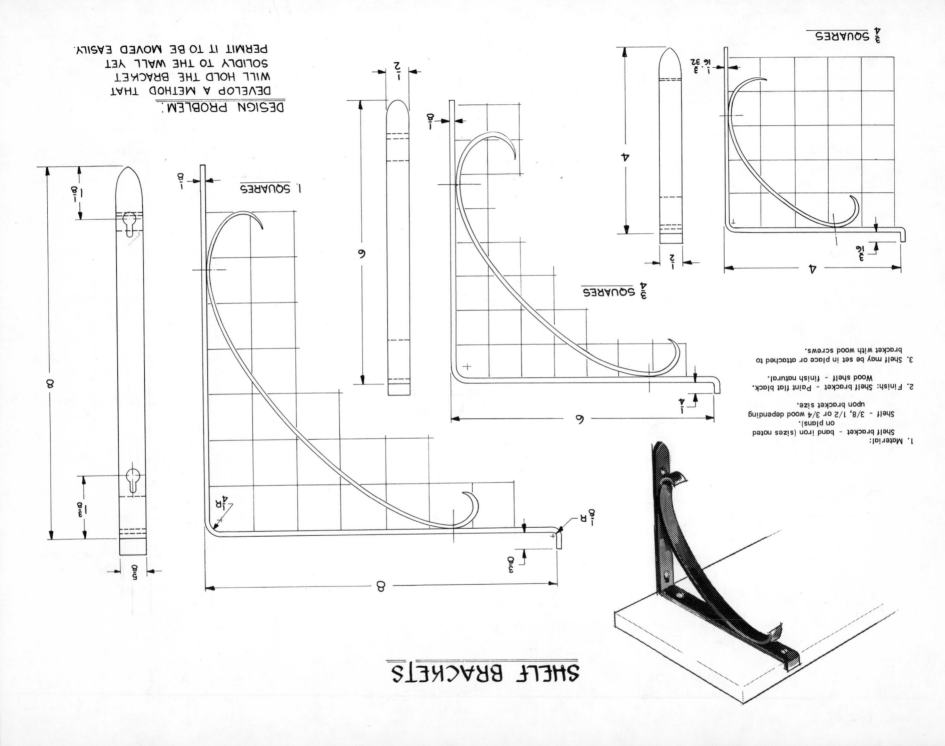

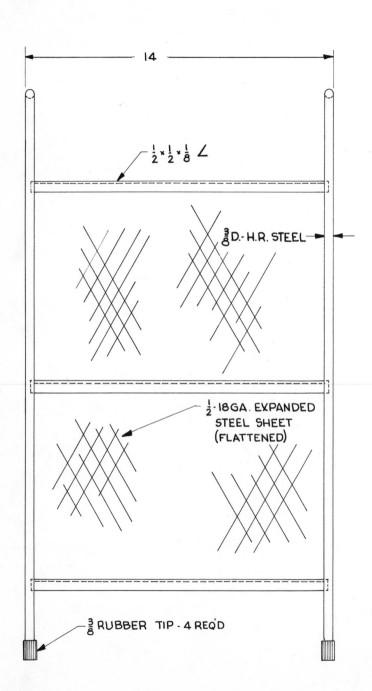

14

$\frac{1}{2} \times \frac{1}{2} \times \frac{1}{8}$ ∠

$\frac{3}{8}$ D.- H.R. STEEL

$\frac{1}{2}$ - 18 GA. EXPANDED STEEL SHEET (FLATTENED)

$\frac{3}{8}$ RUBBER TIP - 4 REQ'D

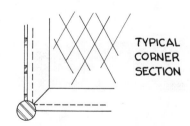

TYPICAL CORNER SECTION

POCKET BOOK STAND

1. Material: Hot rolled steel - sizes as noted.

2. Finish: Paint flat black.

3. Remove all flux from brazed or welded joints and smooth all sharp edges.

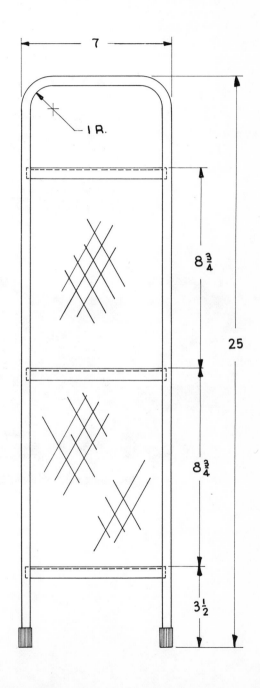

7

I R.

$8\frac{3}{4}$

25

$8\frac{3}{4}$

$3\frac{1}{2}$

NOTES:

1. Material:
   Carriage - Walnut or mahogany with oil finish.
   Cannon - Brass as machined or polished.
   Trunnion bearings - Brass as machined or polished.

2. Assemble carriage with brads and glue.

3. SAFETY: Never attempt to fire a miniature cannon.

The Naval Truck Gun is a replica of the muzzle loading gun found on most naval vessels during the 18th century. They were manufactured in a number of sizes from the one pounder (about a 2 inch bore) up to 24 pounders.

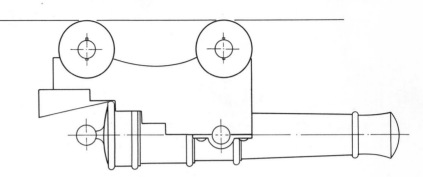

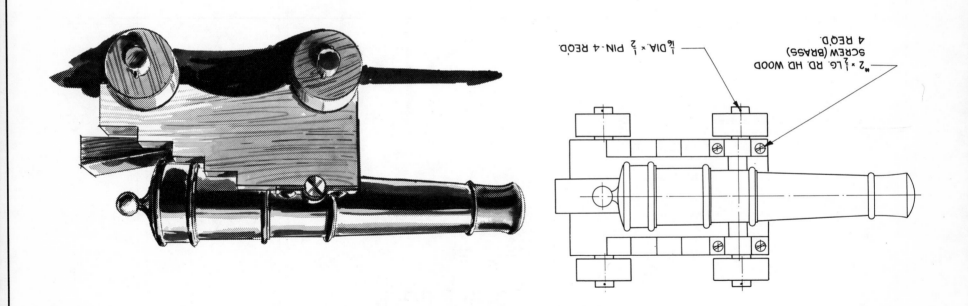

#2 × ⅞ LG. RD. HD. WOOD
SCREW (BRASS)
4 REQ'D.

¹⁄₁₆ DIA × ½ PIN-4 REQ'D.

NAVAL TRUCK GUN

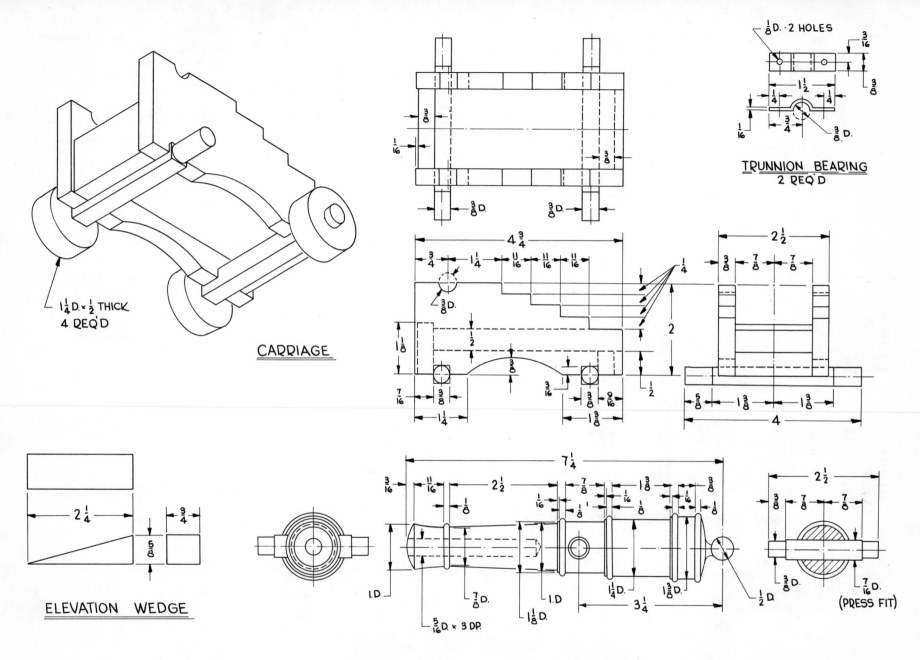

CARRIAGE

TRUNNION BEARING
2 REQ'D

$1\frac{1}{4}$ D. × $\frac{1}{2}$ THICK
4 REQ'D

ELEVATION WEDGE

CANNON

(PRESS FIT)

WEATHER VANES

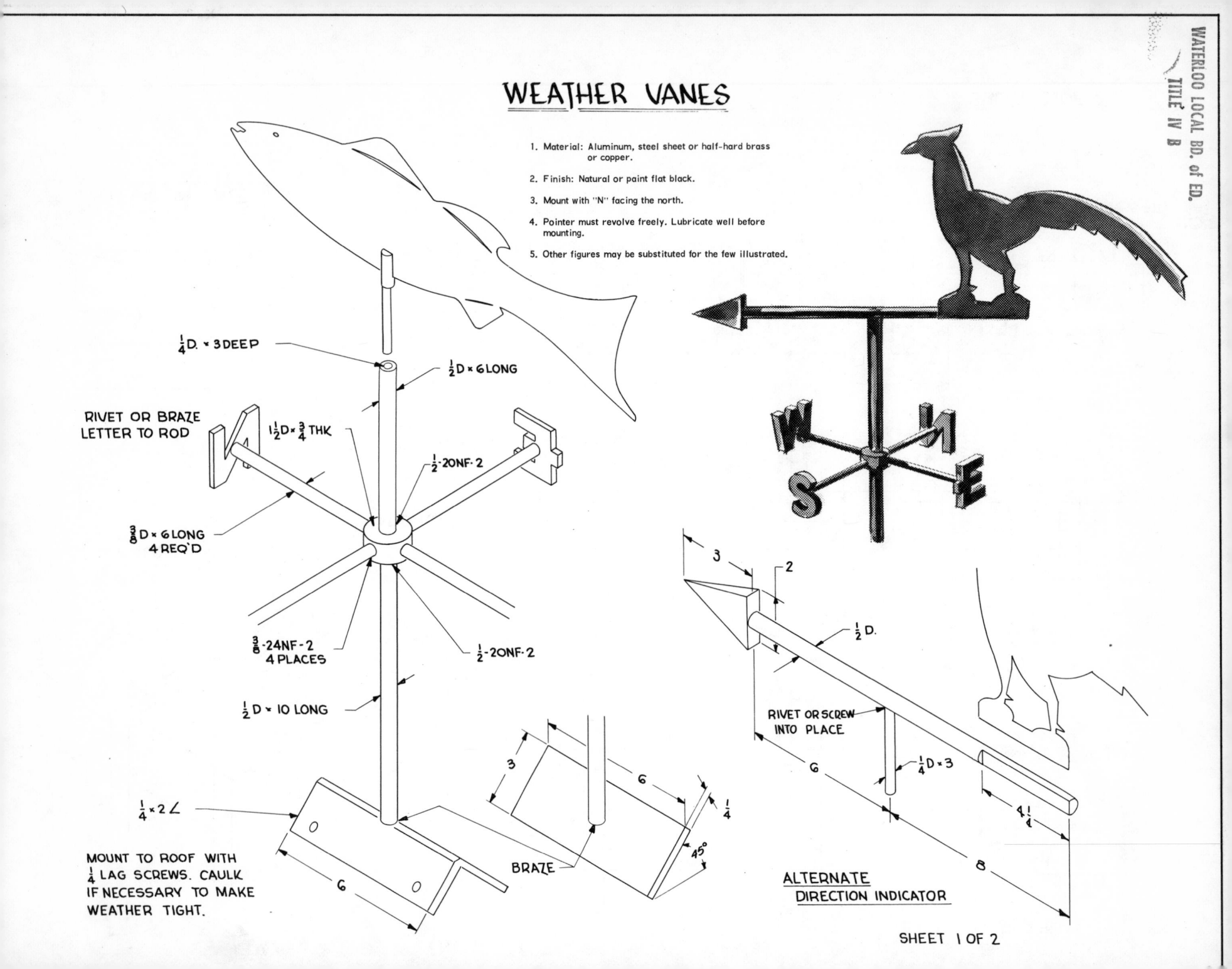

1. Material: Aluminum, steel sheet or half-hard brass or copper.

2. Finish: Natural or paint flat black.

3. Mount with "N" facing the north.

4. Pointer must revolve freely. Lubricate well before mounting.

5. Other figures may be substituted for the few illustrated.

¼ D. × 3 DEEP

½ D × 6 LONG

RIVET OR BRAZE
LETTER TO ROD

1½ D × ¾ THK

½-20NF-2

⅜ D × 6 LONG
4 REQ'D

⅜-24NF-2
4 PLACES

½-20NF-2

½ D × 10 LONG

¼ × 2 ∠

MOUNT TO ROOF WITH
¼ LAG SCREWS. CAULK
IF NECESSARY TO MAKE
WEATHER TIGHT.

6

3

6

¼

45°

BRAZE

3

2

½ D.

RIVET OR SCREW
INTO PLACE

6

¼ D × 3

4¼

8

ALTERNATE
DIRECTION INDICATOR

SHEET 1 OF 2

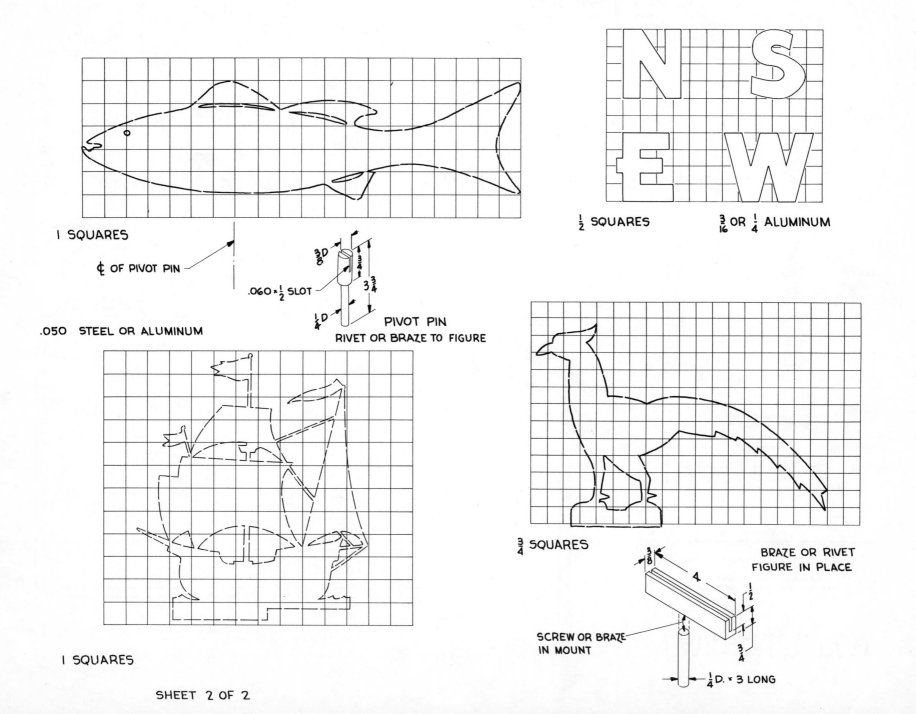

I SQUARES

¢ OF PIVOT PIN

.050 STEEL OR ALUMINUM

.060 × ½ SLOT

⅜ D

3¾

¼ D

PIVOT PIN
RIVET OR BRAZE TO FIGURE

I SQUARES

SHEET 2 OF 2

½ SQUARES   3/16 OR ¼ ALUMINUM

¾ SQUARES

BRAZE OR RIVET
FIGURE IN PLACE

4

½

¾

⅜

SCREW OR BRAZE
IN MOUNT

¼ D. × 3 LONG

PATIO DUST PAN

1. Material: Body - .032 embossed aluminum sheet *.
   Handle - 1/8 x 3/4 aluminum bar *.

2. Finish: Natural

*Reynolds Metals Company Do-It-Yourself aluminum available at most hardware stores.

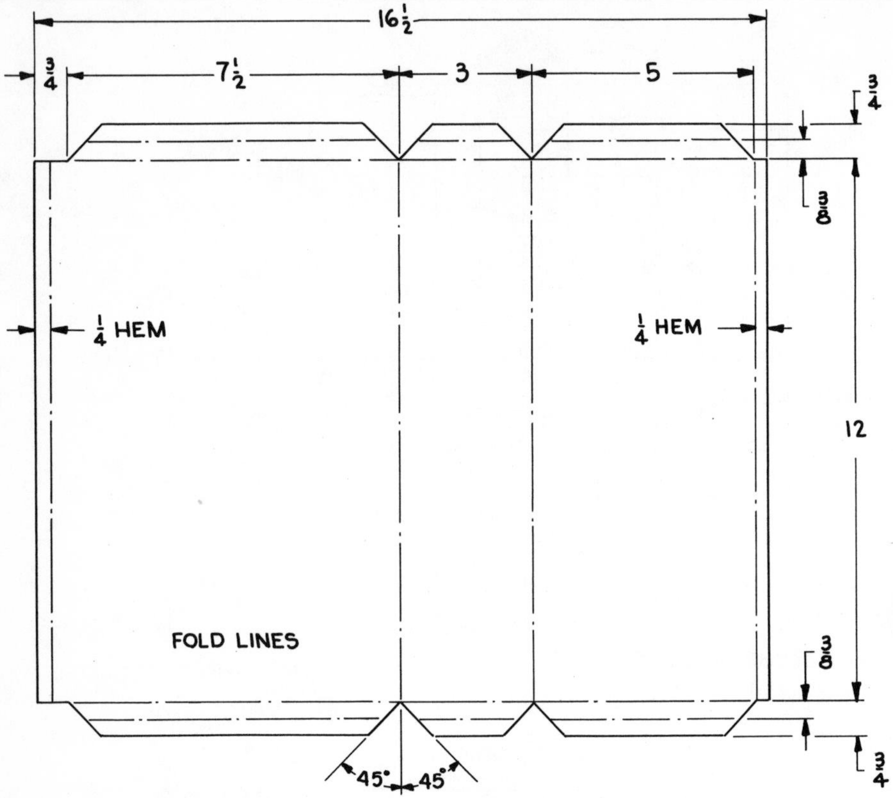

16 1/2
3/4
7 1/2
3
5
3/4
3/8
1/4 HEM
1/4 HEM
12
FOLD LINES
3/8
3/4
45°
45°

PAN

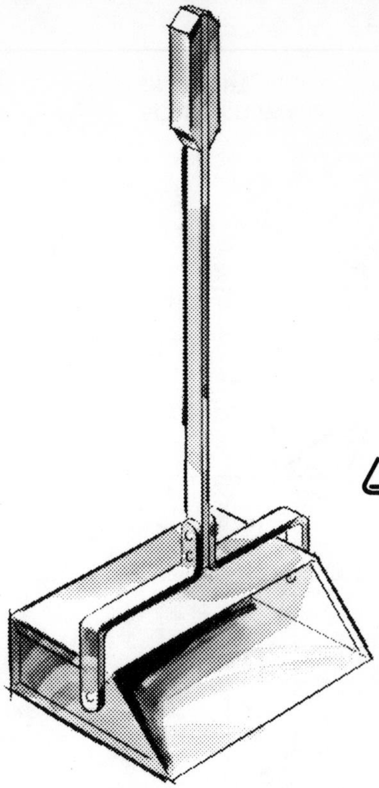

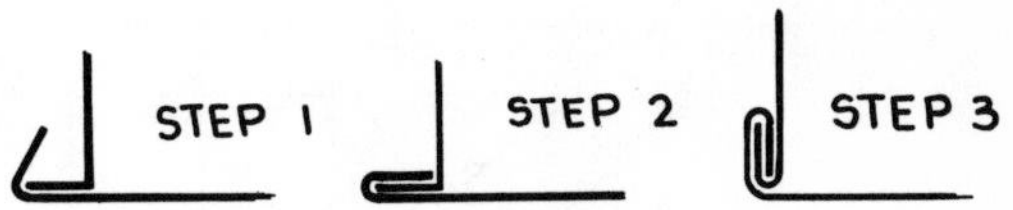

STEP 1
STEP 2
STEP 3

SEAM DETAILS

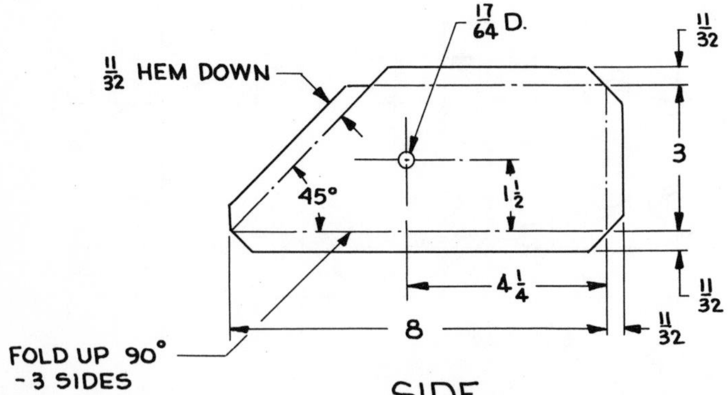

17/64 D.
11/32
11/32 HEM DOWN
3
45°
1 1/2
11/32
4 1/4
8
11/32
FOLD UP 90° - 3 SIDES

SIDE

2 REQ'D - 1 RH
1 LH

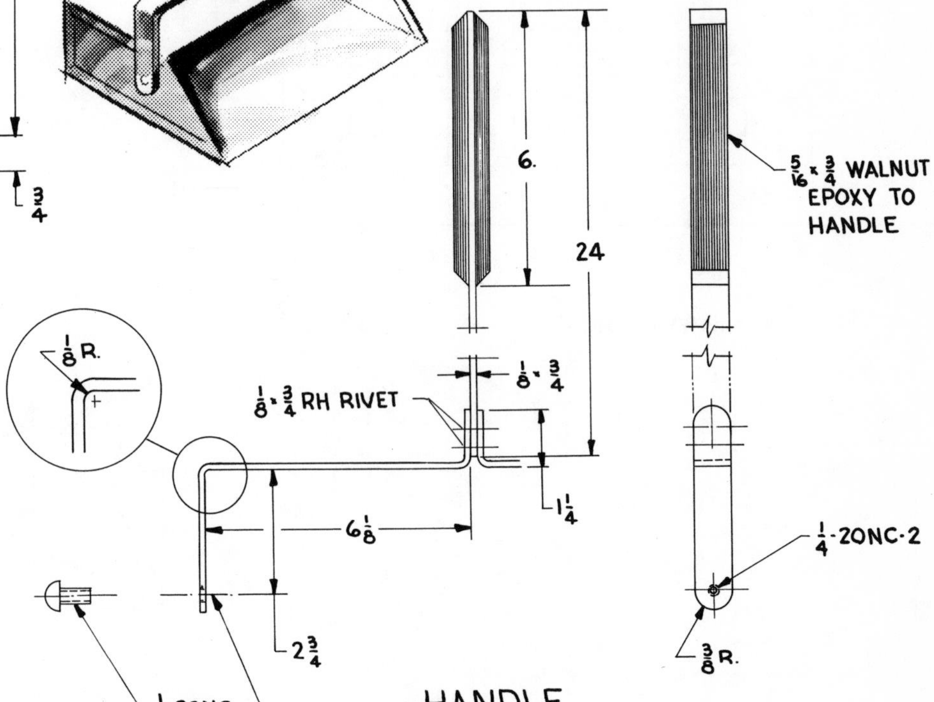

6.
24
5/16 x 3/4 WALNUT EPOXY TO HANDLE
1/8 R.
1/8 x 3/4
1/8 x 3/4 RH RIVET
1 1/4
6 1/8
1/4-20NC-2
2 3/4
3/8 R.
1/4-20NC x 1/2 R.H. SCREW
USE WASHER SPACERS AS NEEDED

HANDLE

MODERN STOOL

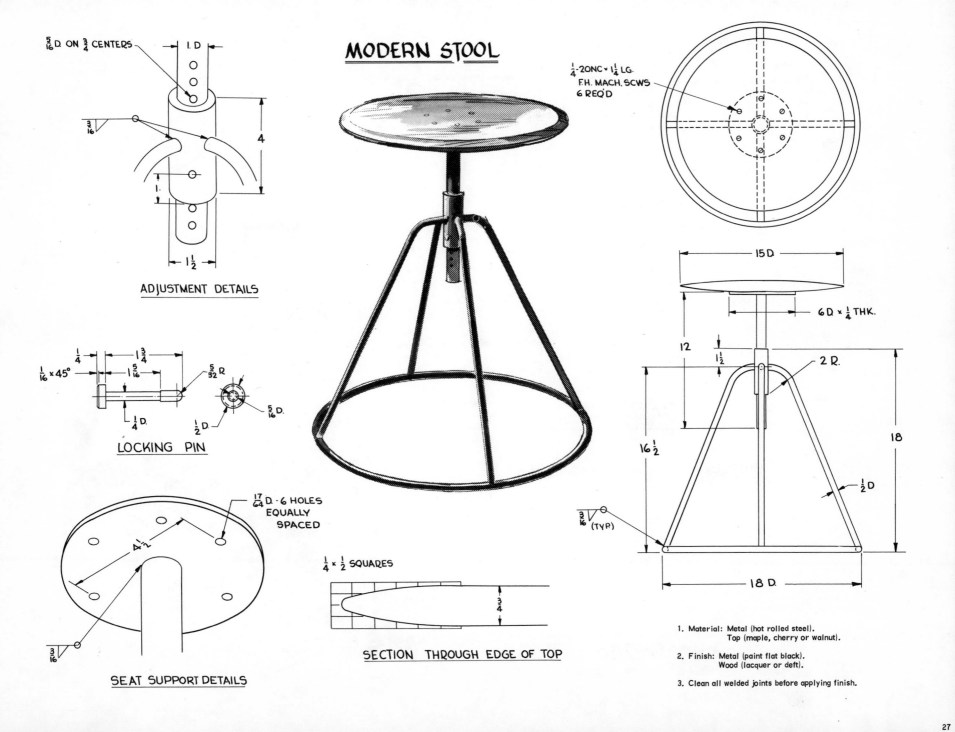

ADJUSTMENT DETAILS

$\frac{5}{16}$ D. ON $\frac{3}{4}$ CENTERS

1. D

$\frac{3}{16}$

4

1.

$1\frac{1}{2}$

LOCKING PIN

$\frac{1}{16} \times 45°$

$\frac{1}{4}$

$1\frac{3}{4}$

$1\frac{5}{16}$

$\frac{5}{32}$ R

$\frac{1}{4}$ D.

$\frac{1}{2}$ D.

$\frac{5}{16}$ D.

SEAT SUPPORT DETAILS

$\frac{17}{64}$ D - 6 HOLES EQUALLY SPACED

$4\frac{1}{2}$

$\frac{3}{16}$

SECTION THROUGH EDGE OF TOP

$\frac{1}{4} \times \frac{1}{2}$ SQUARES

$\frac{3}{4}$

$\frac{1}{4}$-20NC × $1\frac{1}{4}$ LG.
F.H. MACH. SCWS
6 REQ'D

15 D

6 D × $\frac{1}{4}$ THK.

12

$1\frac{1}{2}$

2 R.

18

$16\frac{1}{2}$

$\frac{1}{2}$ D

$\frac{3}{16}$ (TYP)

18 D.

1. Material: Metal (hot rolled steel).
    Top (maple, cherry or walnut).

2. Finish: Metal (paint flat black).
    Wood (lacquer or deft).

3. Clean all welded joints before applying finish.

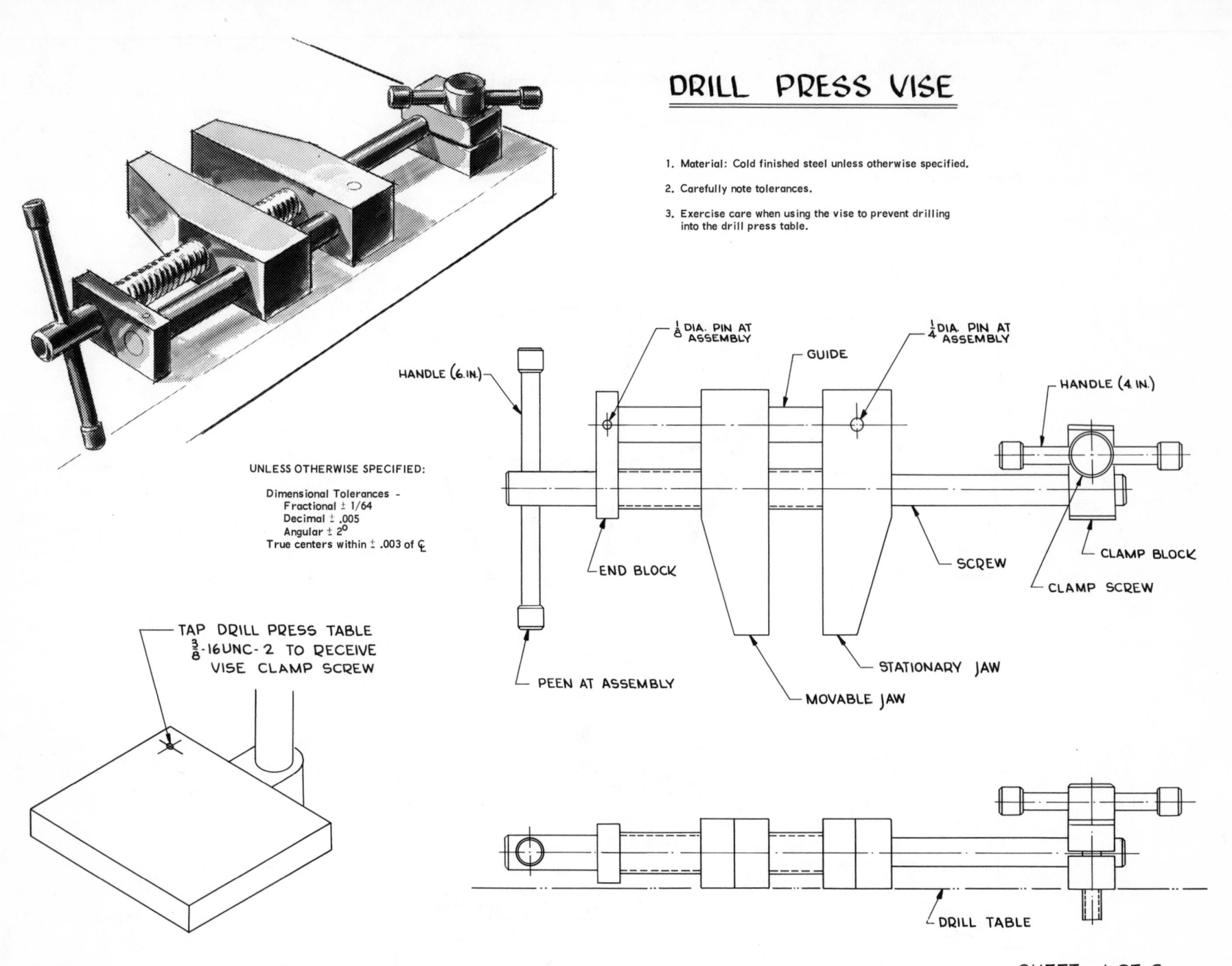

DRILL PRESS VISE

1. Material: Cold finished steel unless otherwise specified.

2. Carefully note tolerances.

3. Exercise care when using the vise to prevent drilling into the drill press table.

UNLESS OTHERWISE SPECIFIED:

Dimensional Tolerances -
Fractional ± 1/64
Decimal ± .005
Angular ± 2°
True centers within ± .003 of ₵

$\frac{1}{8}$ DIA. PIN AT ASSEMBLY

$\frac{1}{4}$ DIA. PIN AT ASSEMBLY

GUIDE

HANDLE (6.IN.)

HANDLE (4.IN.)

END BLOCK

SCREW

CLAMP BLOCK

CLAMP SCREW

PEEN AT ASSEMBLY

STATIONARY JAW

MOVABLE JAW

TAP DRILL PRESS TABLE
$\frac{3}{8}$-16UNC-2 TO RECEIVE
VISE CLAMP SCREW

DRILL TABLE

SHEET 1 OF 2

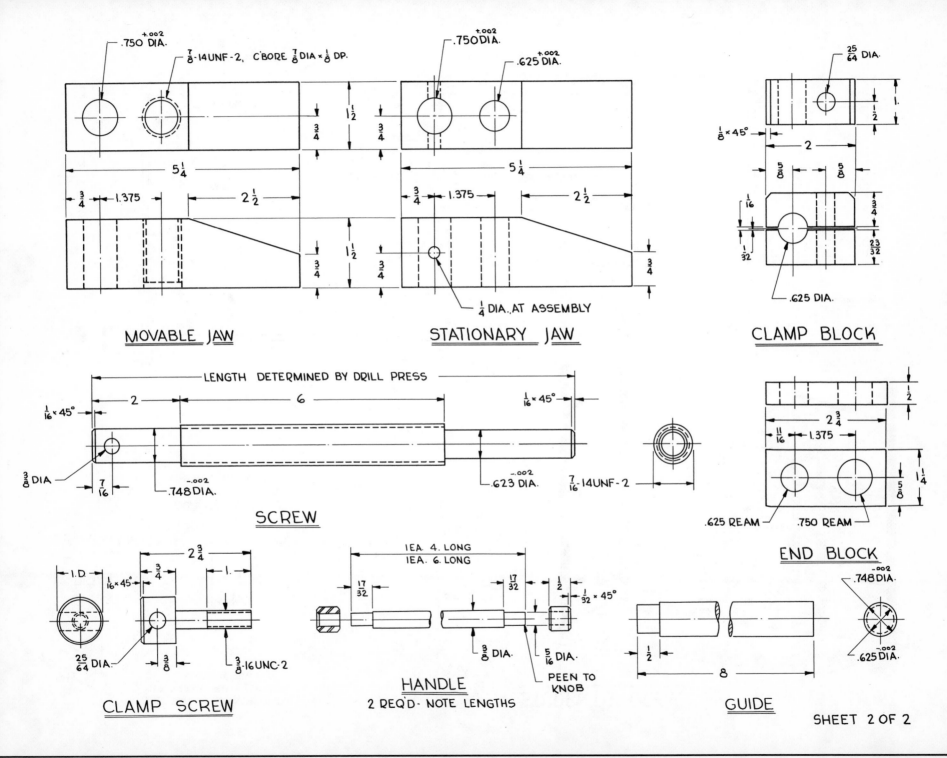

MOVABLE JAW

STATIONARY JAW

CLAMP BLOCK

SCREW

END BLOCK

CLAMP SCREW

HANDLE
2 REQ'D. NOTE LENGTHS

GUIDE

SHEET 2 OF 2

29

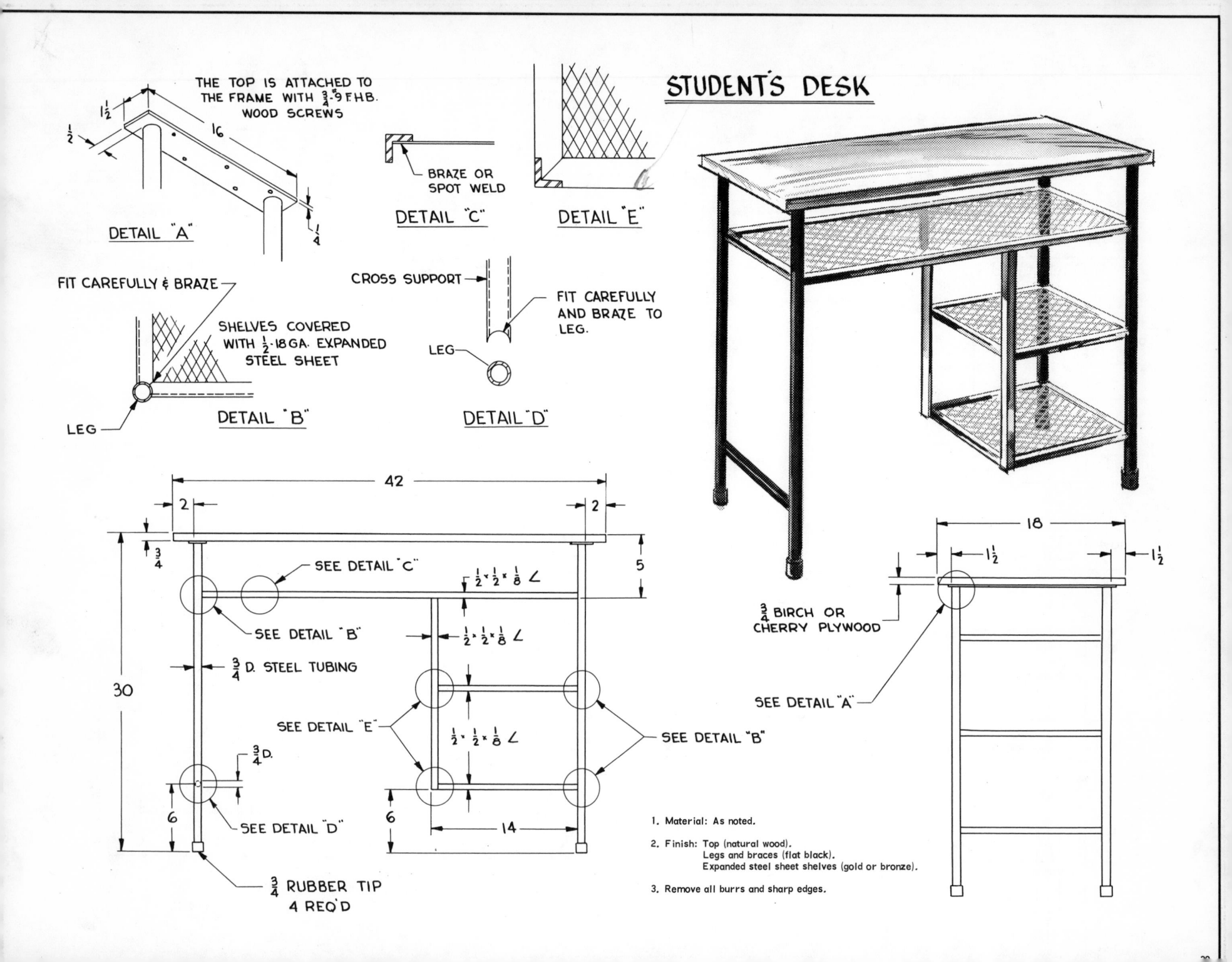

THE TOP IS ATTACHED TO
THE FRAME WITH $\frac{3}{4}$ #9 F.H.B.
WOOD SCREWS

1½

½

16

¼

DETAIL "A"

BRAZE OR
SPOT WELD

DETAIL "C"

DETAIL "E"

STUDENT'S DESK

FIT CAREFULLY & BRAZE

SHELVES COVERED
WITH ½-18 GA. EXPANDED
STEEL SHEET

CROSS SUPPORT

FIT CAREFULLY
AND BRAZE TO
LEG.

LEG

LEG

DETAIL "B"

DETAIL "D"

42

2

2

SEE DETAIL "C"

5

$\frac{1}{2} \times \frac{1}{2} \times \frac{1}{8}$ ∠

$\frac{3}{4}$

SEE DETAIL "B"

$\frac{1}{2} \times \frac{1}{2} \times \frac{1}{8}$ ∠

$\frac{3}{4}$ D. STEEL TUBING

30

SEE DETAIL "E"

$\frac{1}{2} \times \frac{1}{2} \times \frac{1}{8}$ ∠

SEE DETAIL "B"

$\frac{3}{4}$ D.

$\frac{3}{4}$ BIRCH OR
CHERRY PLYWOOD

SEE DETAIL "D"

6

6

14

18

1½

1½

SEE DETAIL "A"

$\frac{3}{4}$ RUBBER TIP
4 REQ'D

1. Material: As noted.

2. Finish: Top (natural wood).
   Legs and braces (flat black).
   Expanded steel sheet shelves (gold or bronze).

3. Remove all burrs and sharp edges.

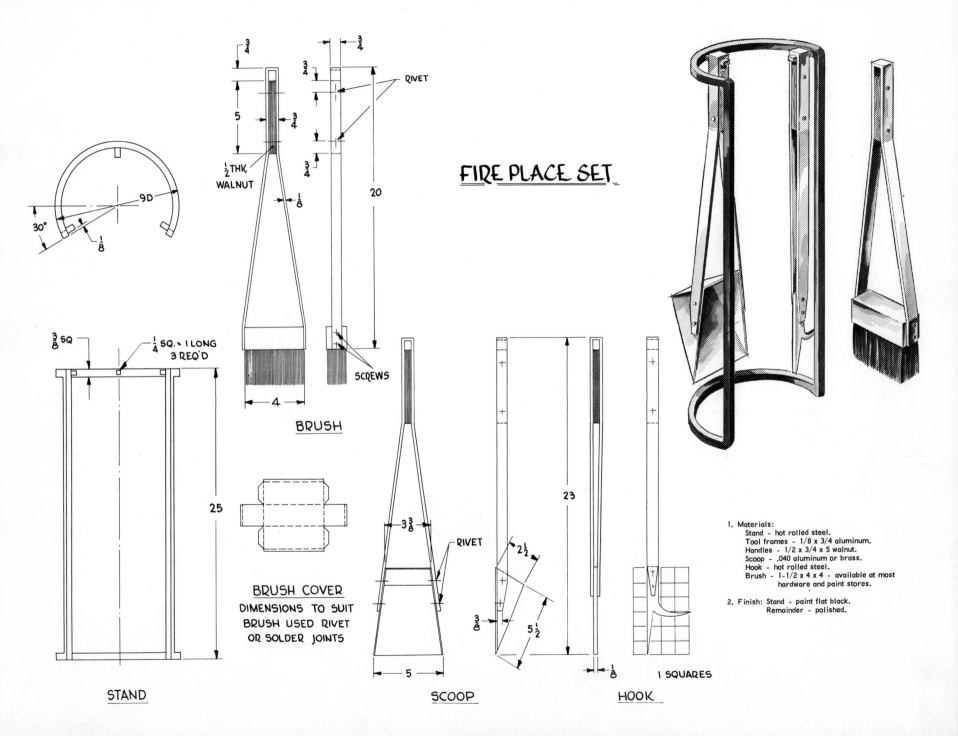

FIRE PLACE SET

9D

30°

1/8

STAND

3/8 SQ

1/4 SQ. × 1 LONG
3 REQ'D

25

3/4

3/4

5

3/4

1/8

1/2 THK.
WALNUT

3/4

3/4

3/4

RIVET

20

SCREWS

4

BRUSH

BRUSH COVER
DIMENSIONS TO SUIT
BRUSH USED RIVET
OR SOLDER JOINTS

3 3/8

RIVET

5

SCOOP

23

2 1/2

3/8

5 1/2

1/8

HOOK

1 SQUARES

1. Materials:
   Stand - hot rolled steel.
   Tool frames - 1/8 x 3/4 aluminum.
   Handles - 1/2 x 3/4 x 5 walnut.
   Scoop - .040 aluminum or brass.
   Hook - hot rolled steel.
   Brush - 1-1/2 x 4 x 4 - available at most
           hardware and paint stores.

2. Finish: Stand - paint flat black.
   Remainder - polished.

CONTEMPORARY TRIVETS

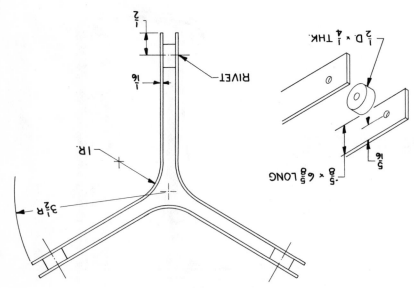

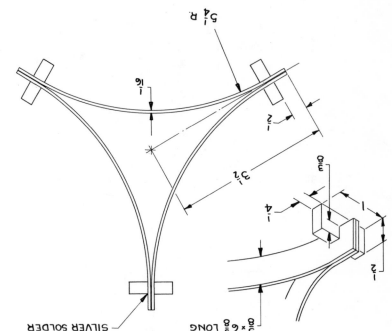

A TRIVET is a device used to prevent hot dishes, pans, etc. from damaging the surface of a table.

1. Material: Half-hard brass, copper or aluminum.

2. Finish: As desired.

3. Use considerable care when silver soldering or riveting; otherwise, the finished trivet will not sit square and may allow the hot dish to topple over.

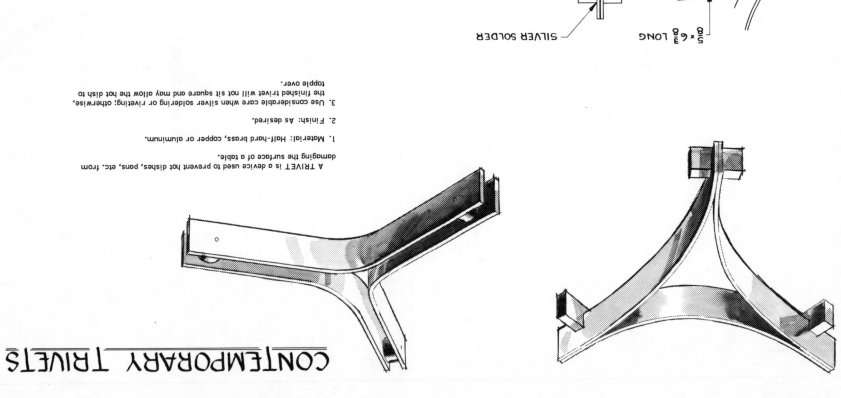

PEN HOLDER BASE

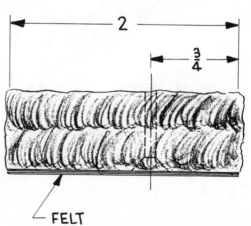

1. Material: Cold finished steel.

2. Finish: Polish deposited braze material.

3. Remove all burrs and sharp edges.

4. Pen and pen holder available from most school shop supply houses.

BRASS ROD DEPOSITED IN BEADS OF VARIOUS SIZES BY BRAZING

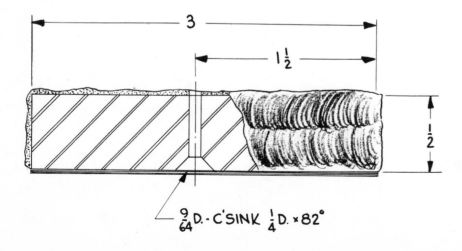

3

$1\frac{1}{2}$

$\frac{1}{2}$

$\frac{9}{64}$ D. - C'SINK $\frac{1}{4}$ D. × 82°

2

$\frac{3}{4}$

FELT

SHOE SCRAPER

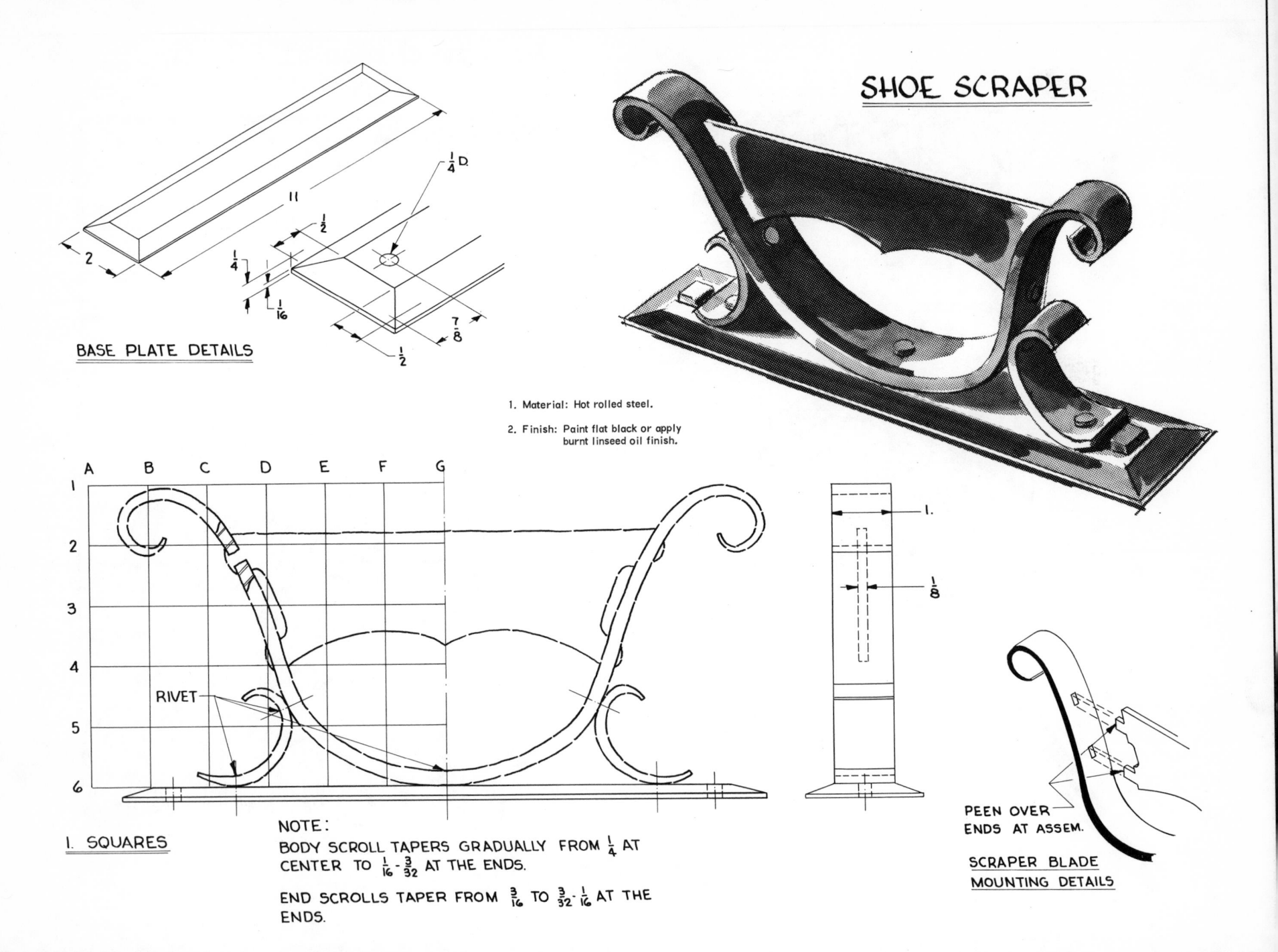

BASE PLATE DETAILS

11

2

¼ D.

½

¼

1/16

7/8

½

1. Material: Hot rolled steel.

2. Finish: Paint flat black or apply burnt linseed oil finish.

1. SQUARES

RIVET

1.

⅛

NOTE:
BODY SCROLL TAPERS GRADUALLY FROM ¼ AT CENTER TO 1/16 - 3/32 AT THE ENDS.

END SCROLLS TAPER FROM 3/16 TO 3/32 - 1/16 AT THE ENDS.

PEEN OVER ENDS AT ASSEM.

SCRAPER BLADE MOUNTING DETAILS

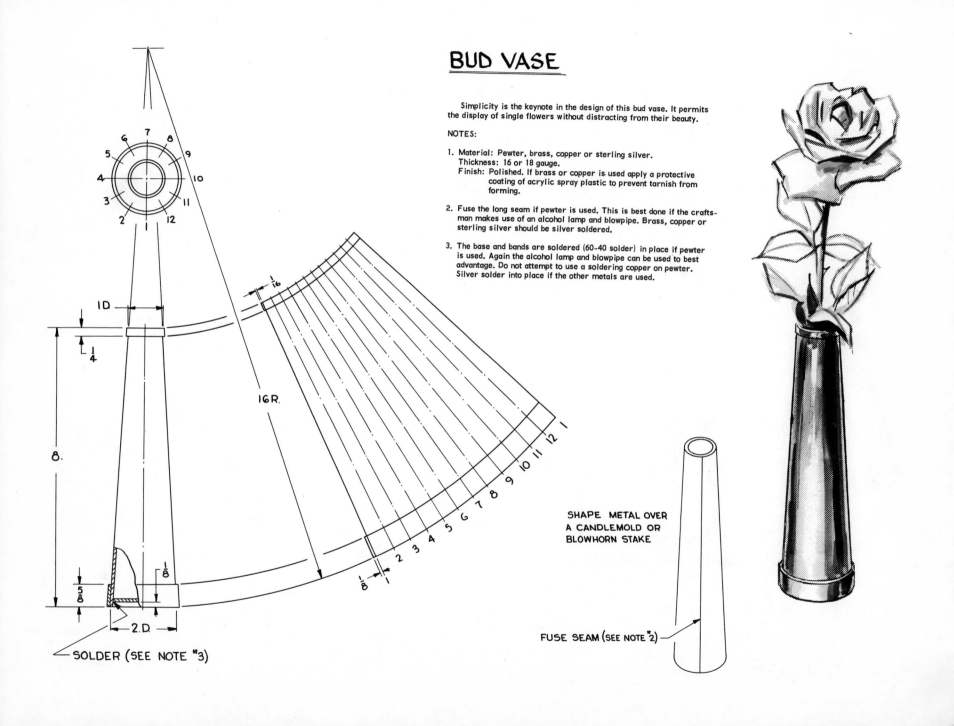

BUD VASE

Simplicity is the keynote in the design of this bud vase. It permits the display of single flowers without distracting from their beauty.

NOTES:

1. Material: Pewter, brass, copper or sterling silver.
   Thickness: 16 or 18 gauge.
   Finish: Polished. If brass or copper is used apply a protective coating of acrylic spray plastic to prevent tarnish from forming.

2. Fuse the long seam if pewter is used. This is best done if the craftsman makes use of an alcohol lamp and blowpipe. Brass, copper or sterling silver should be silver soldered.

3. The base and bands are soldered (60-40 solder) in place if pewter is used. Again the alcohol lamp and blowpipe can be used to best advantage. Do not attempt to use a soldering copper on pewter. Silver solder into place if the other metals are used.

SHAPE METAL OVER A CANDLEMOLD OR BLOWHORN STAKE

FUSE SEAM (SEE NOTE #2)

SOLDER (SEE NOTE #3)

COFFEE SERVER

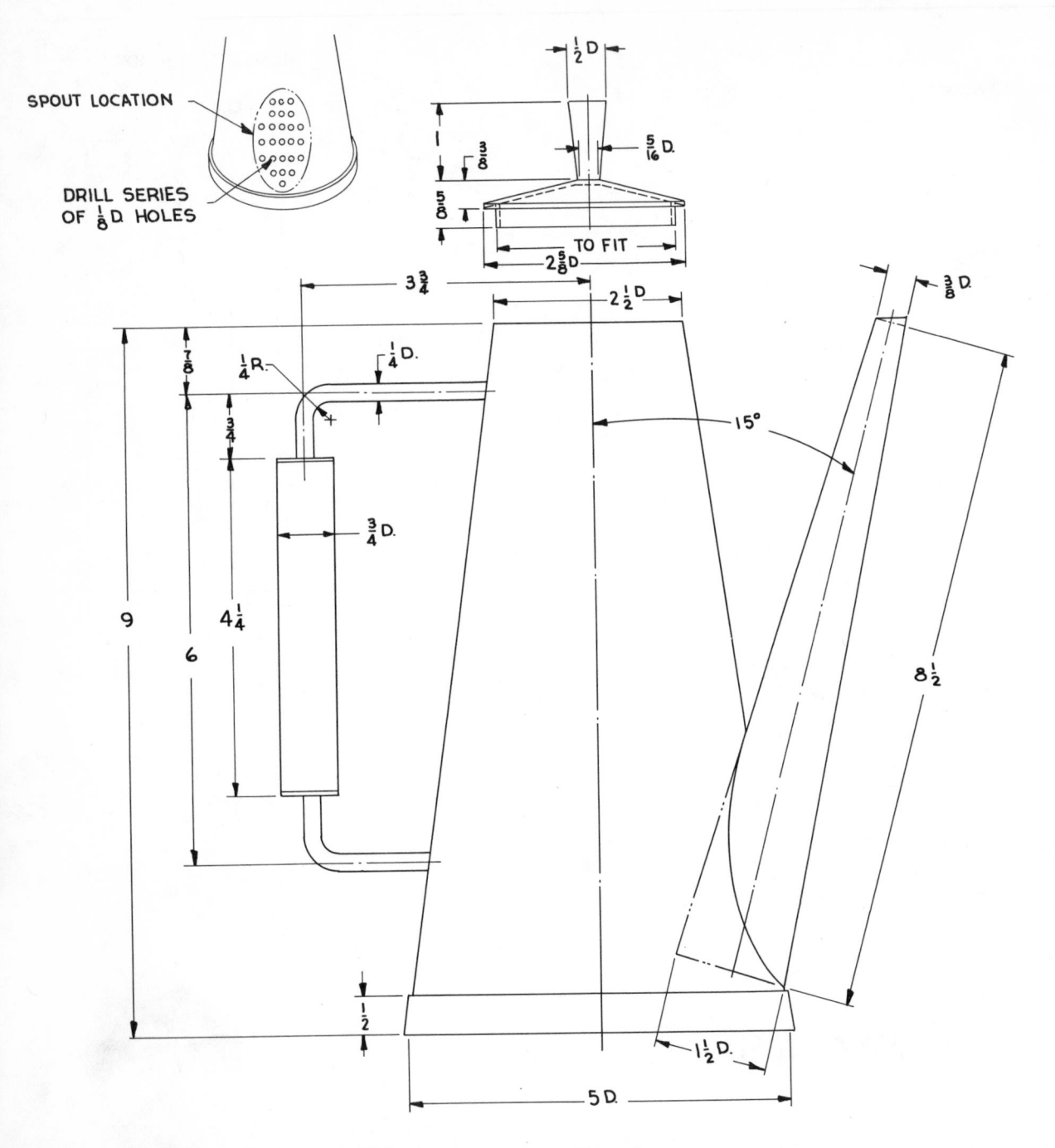

SPOUT LOCATION

DRILL SERIES
OF $\frac{1}{8}$ D HOLES

$\frac{1}{2}$ D

$\frac{5}{16}$ D.

1

$\frac{3}{8}$

$\frac{5}{8}$

TO FIT

$2\frac{3}{8}$ D.

$3\frac{3}{4}$

$2\frac{1}{2}$ D

$\frac{3}{8}$ D.

$\frac{1}{4}$ R.

$\frac{1}{4}$ D.

15°

$\frac{7}{8}$

$\frac{3}{4}$

$\frac{3}{4}$ D.

9

6

$4\frac{1}{4}$

$8\frac{1}{2}$

$\frac{1}{2}$

$1\frac{1}{2}$ D.

5 D.

This project is for the advanced metals student. The dimensions and the basic design are for reference purposes only. It is hoped that the student will use these ideas and develop an original design.

Should the dimensions and basic design be used the student will find himself confronted with several challenging problems:

1. Develop the patterns using accepted drafting techniques.

2. Devise a method to attach the handle solidly to the supports.

3. Decide what metal or combination of metals (16 ga.) will present the most attractive appearance.

MAGAZINE RACK TABLE

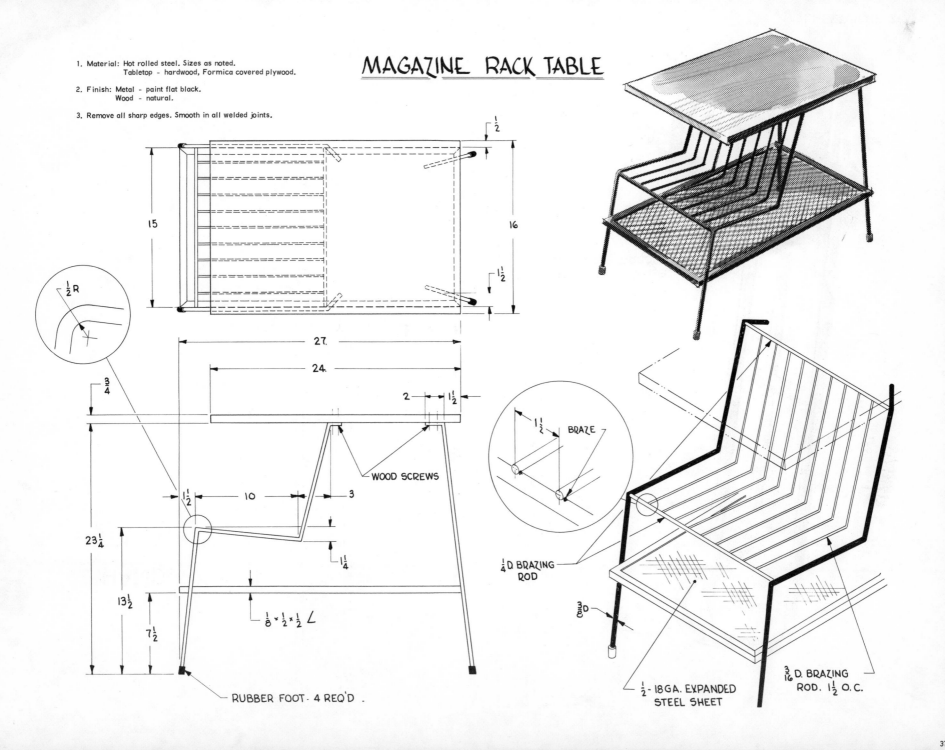

1. Material: Hot rolled steel. Sizes as noted.
   Tabletop - hardwood, Formica covered plywood.

2. Finish: Metal - paint flat black.
   Wood - natural.

3. Remove all sharp edges. Smooth in all welded joints.

$\frac{1}{2}$R

15

16

$\frac{1}{2}$

$1\frac{1}{2}$

27.

24.

2

$1\frac{1}{2}$

$\frac{3}{4}$

WOOD SCREWS

$1\frac{1}{2}$

10

3

$23\frac{1}{4}$

$1\frac{1}{4}$

$13\frac{1}{2}$

$7\frac{1}{2}$

$\frac{1}{8} \times \frac{1}{2} \times \frac{1}{2}$ L

RUBBER FOOT - 4 REQ'D.

$1\frac{1}{2}$

BRAZE

$\frac{1}{4}$ D BRAZING ROD

$\frac{3}{16}$ D

$\frac{1}{2}$ - 18 GA. EXPANDED STEEL SHEET

$\frac{3}{16}$ D. BRAZING ROD. $1\frac{1}{2}$ O.C.

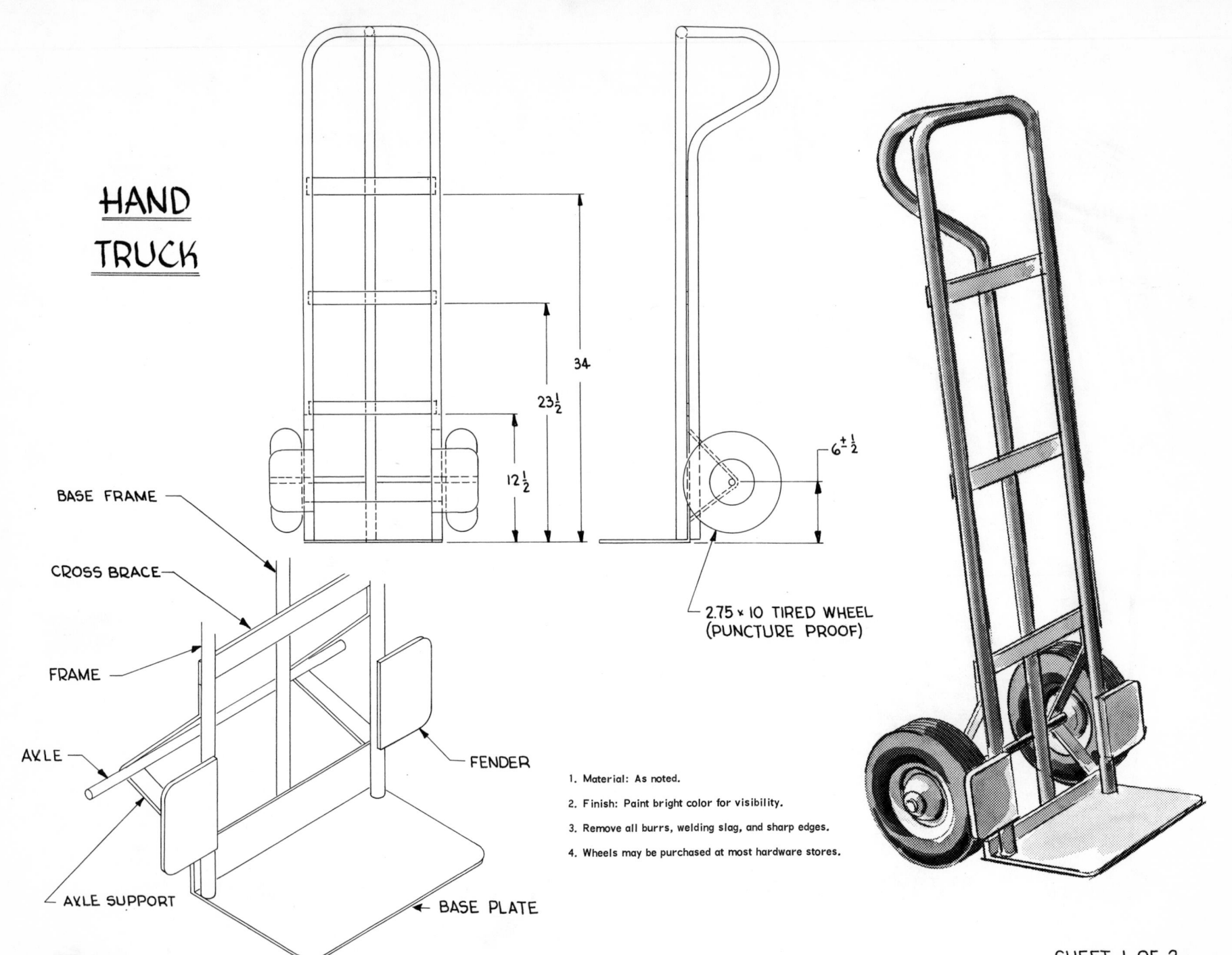

HAND
TRUCK

34

$23\frac{1}{2}$

$12\frac{1}{2}$

$6^{+\frac{1}{2}}$

BASE FRAME

CROSS BRACE

FRAME

AXLE

AXLE SUPPORT

FENDER

BASE PLATE

2.75 × 10 TIRED WHEEL
(PUNCTURE PROOF)

1. Material: As noted.

2. Finish: Paint bright color for visibility.

3. Remove all burrs, welding slag, and sharp edges.

4. Wheels may be purchased at most hardware stores.

SHEET 1 OF 2

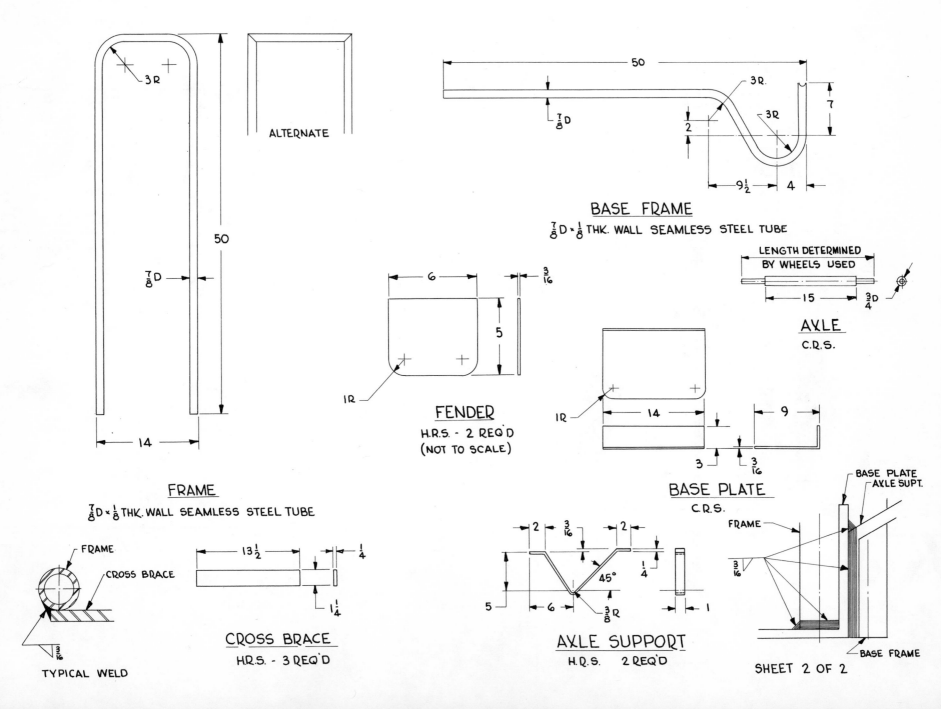

ALTERNATE

3R

50

$\frac{7}{8}$D

14

FRAME

$\frac{7}{8}$D × $\frac{1}{8}$ THK. WALL SEAMLESS STEEL TUBE

FRAME

CROSS BRACE

$\frac{3}{16}$

TYPICAL WELD

13$\frac{1}{2}$

$\frac{1}{4}$

1$\frac{1}{4}$

CROSS BRACE

H.R.S. - 3 REQ'D

50

3R

3R

3R

7

2

9$\frac{1}{2}$

4

$\frac{7}{8}$D

BASE FRAME

$\frac{7}{8}$D × $\frac{1}{8}$ THK. WALL SEAMLESS STEEL TUBE

6

$\frac{3}{16}$

5

1R

FENDER

H.R.S. - 2 REQ'D

(NOT TO SCALE)

LENGTH DETERMINED
BY WHEELS USED

15

$\frac{3}{4}$D

AXLE

C.R.S.

1R

14

9

3

$\frac{3}{16}$

BASE PLATE

C.R.S.

2

$\frac{3}{16}$

2

$\frac{1}{4}$

45°

5

6

$\frac{3}{8}$R

1

AXLE SUPPORT

H.R.S.   2 REQ'D

BASE PLATE

BASE PLATE
AXLE SUPT.

FRAME

$\frac{3}{16}$

BASE FRAME

SHEET 2 OF 2

39

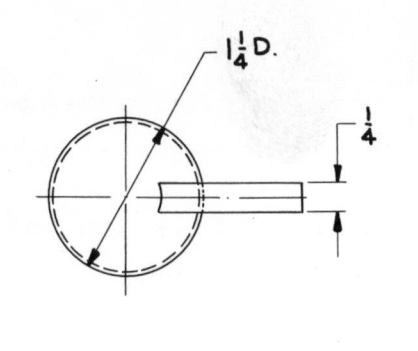

$1\frac{1}{4}$ D.

$\frac{1}{4}$

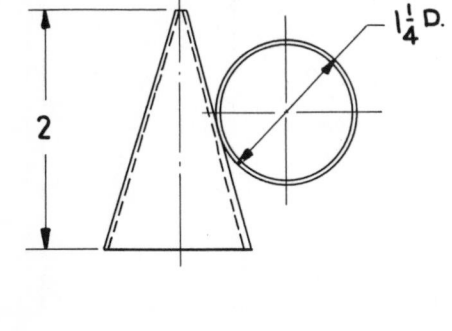

2

$1\frac{1}{4}$ D.

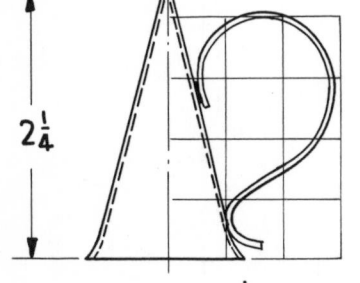

$2\frac{1}{4}$

$\frac{1}{2}$ SQUARES

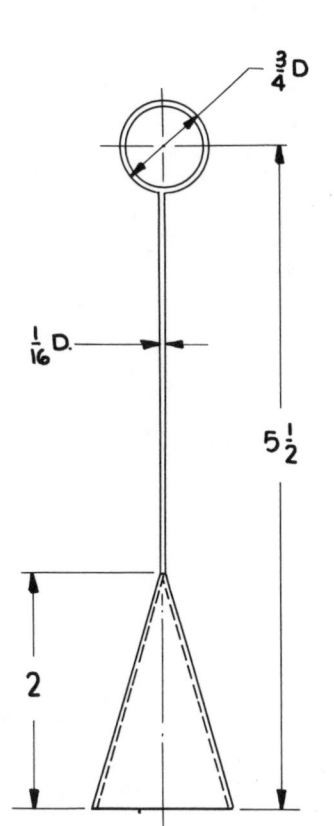

$\frac{3}{4}$ D

$\frac{1}{16}$ D.

$5\frac{1}{2}$

2

CANDLE SNUFFERS

1. Material: 20 ga. copper, brass or pewter.

2. Finish: Polish (spray copper and brass with clear lacquer to prevent oxidation.

3. Handles may be silver soldered or soft soldered to the snuffers.

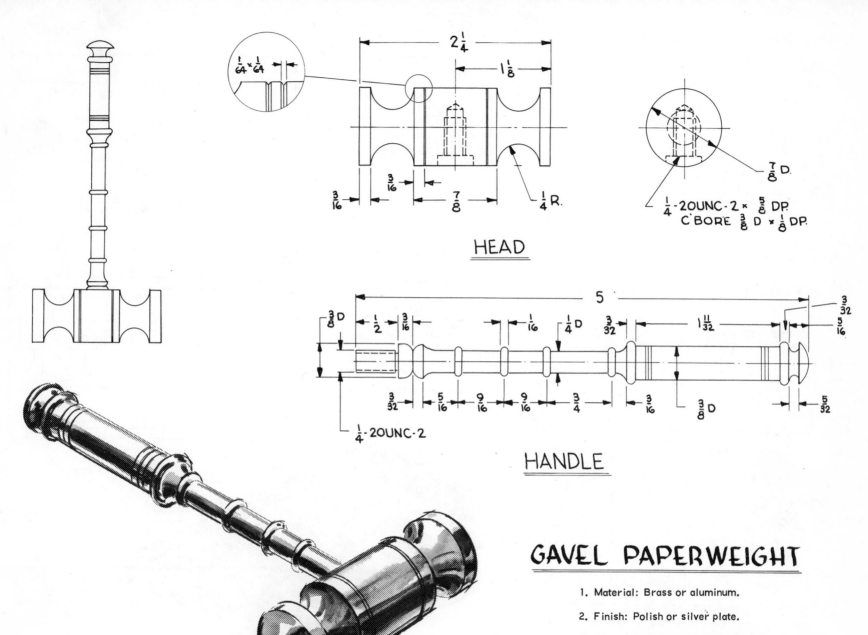

HEAD

$2\frac{1}{4}$

$1\frac{1}{8}$

$\frac{1}{64} \times \frac{1}{64}$

$\frac{3}{16}$

$\frac{3}{16}$

$\frac{7}{8}$

$\frac{1}{4}$ R.

$\frac{7}{8}$ D.

$\frac{1}{4}$ - 20UNC - 2 × $\frac{5}{8}$ DP.
C'BORE $\frac{3}{8}$ D × $\frac{1}{8}$ DP.

HANDLE

5

$\frac{3}{8}$ D

$\frac{1}{2}$

$\frac{3}{16}$

$\frac{1}{16}$

$\frac{1}{4}$ D

$\frac{3}{32}$

$1\frac{11}{32}$

$\frac{3}{32}$

$\frac{5}{16}$

$\frac{3}{32}$

$\frac{5}{16}$

$\frac{9}{16}$

$\frac{9}{16}$

$\frac{3}{4}$

$\frac{3}{16}$

$\frac{3}{8}$ D

$\frac{5}{32}$

$\frac{1}{4}$ - 20UNC - 2

GAVEL PAPERWEIGHT

1. Material: Brass or aluminum.

2. Finish: Polish or silver plate.

3. Remove all burrs and sharp edges.

4. Gavel also makes an ideal gift for retiring president or club officer.

CIVIL WAR GUN

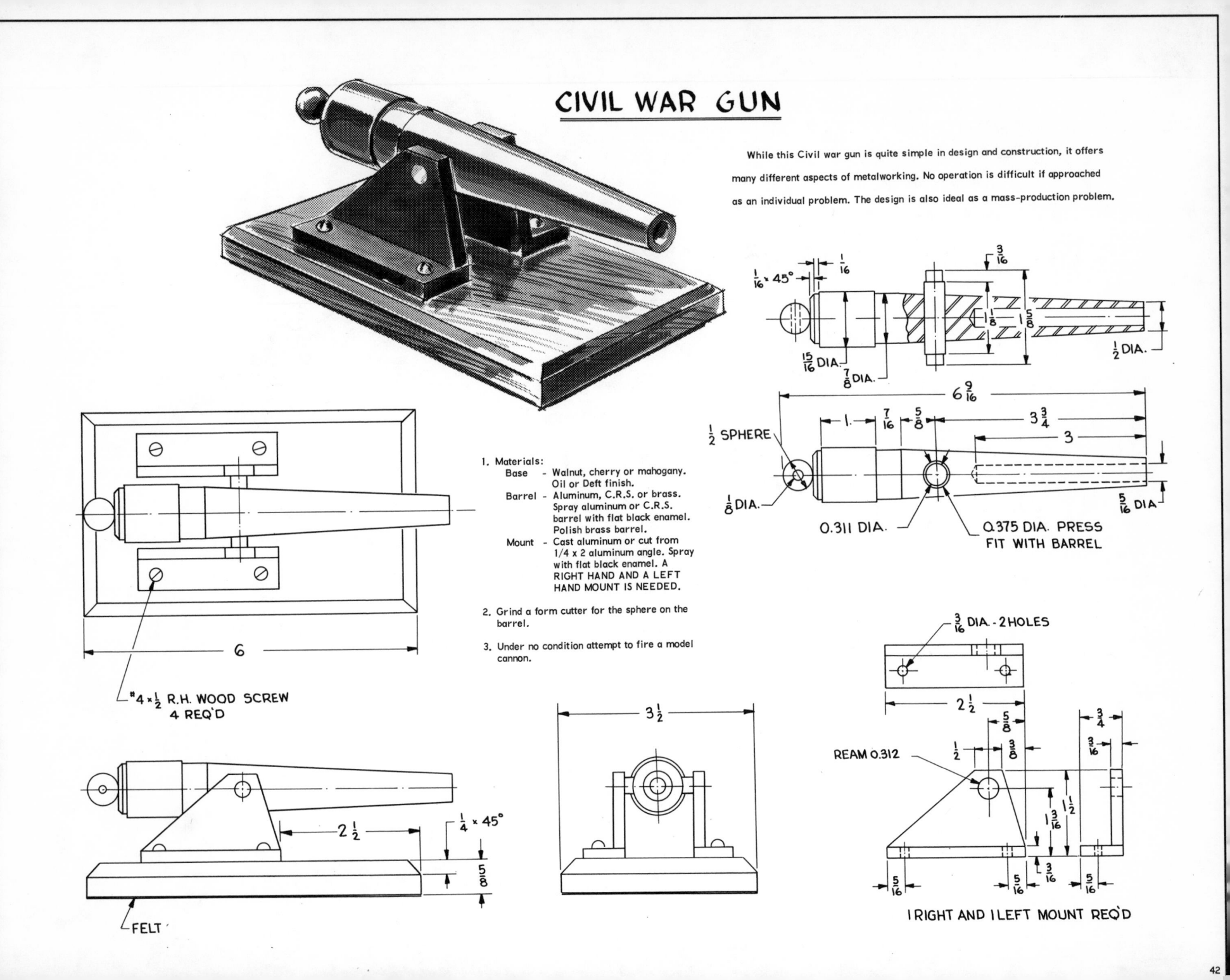

While this Civil war gun is quite simple in design and construction, it offers many different aspects of metalworking. No operation is difficult if approached as an individual problem. The design is also ideal as a mass-production problem.

1. Materials:
   Base - Walnut, cherry or mahogany. Oil or Deft finish.
   Barrel - Aluminum, C.R.S. or brass. Spray aluminum or C.R.S. barrel with flat black enamel. Polish brass barrel.
   Mount - Cast aluminum or cut from 1/4 x 2 aluminum angle. Spray with flat black enamel. A RIGHT HAND AND A LEFT HAND MOUNT IS NEEDED.

2. Grind a form cutter for the sphere on the barrel.

3. Under no condition attempt to fire a model cannon.

#4 x ½ R.H. WOOD SCREW 4 REQ'D

FELT

1 RIGHT AND 1 LEFT MOUNT REQ'D

CONTEMPORARY PATIO TABLE

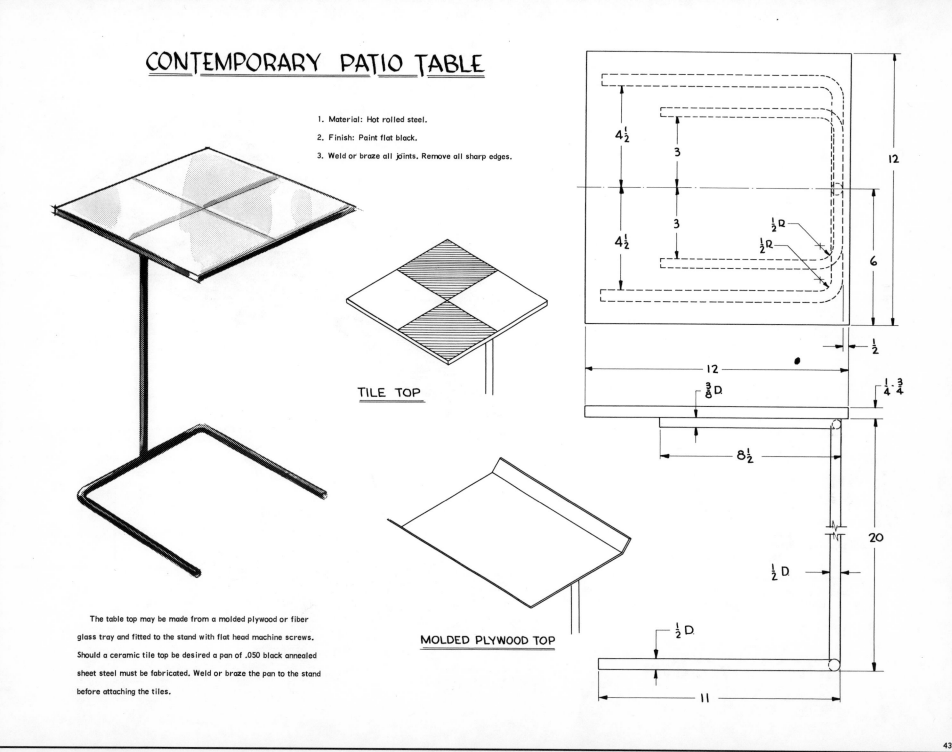

1. Material: Hot rolled steel.

2. Finish: Paint flat black.

3. Weld or braze all joints. Remove all sharp edges.

TILE TOP

MOLDED PLYWOOD TOP

The table top may be made from a molded plywood or fiber glass tray and fitted to the stand with flat head machine screws. Should a ceramic tile top be desired a pan of .050 black annealed sheet steel must be fabricated. Weld or braze the pan to the stand before attaching the tiles.

CHARCOAL SCOOP

$4\frac{3}{4}$

$3\frac{1}{4}$

$4\frac{1}{4}$

$\frac{1}{8} \times \frac{1}{2}$

RIVET

1. Material: Handle - hot rolled steel.
   Scoop - 18 ga. brass or black iron sheet.

2. Finish: Handle - flat black.
   Scoop - polished brass or flat black iron sheet.

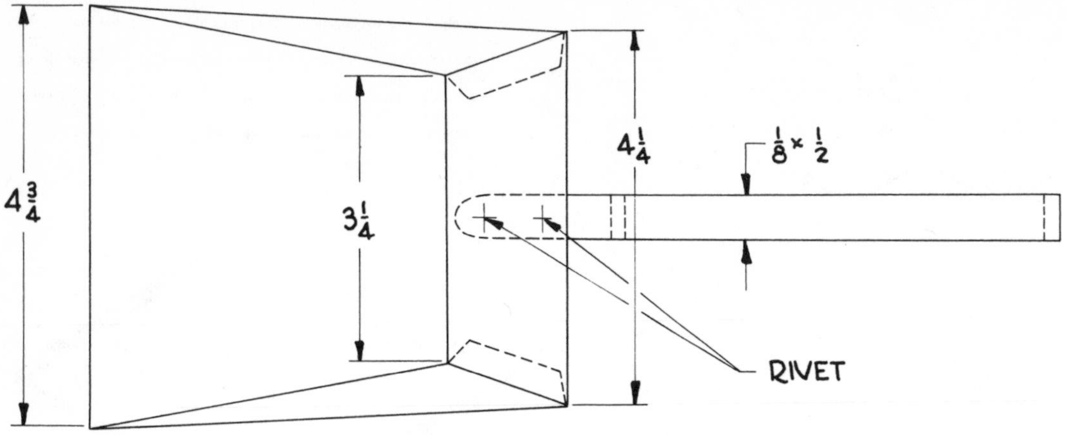

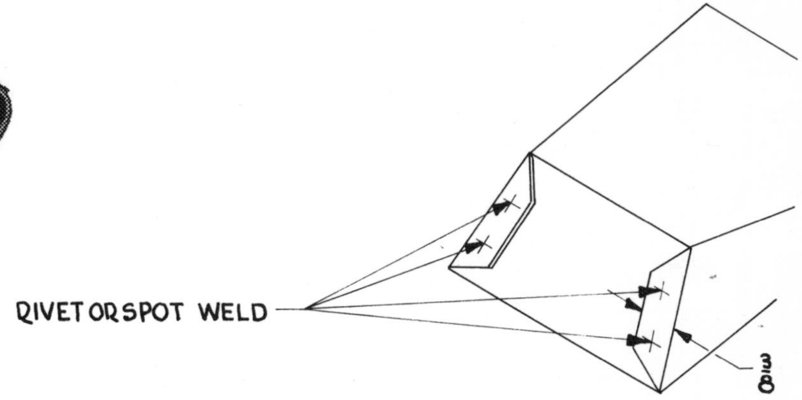

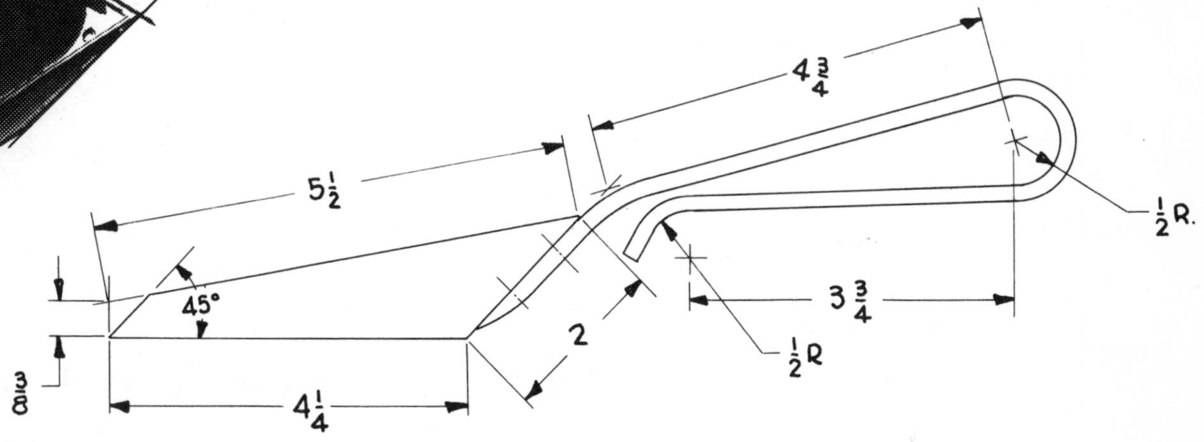

RIVET OR SPOT WELD

$\frac{3}{8}$

$4\frac{3}{4}$

$\frac{1}{2}$ R.

$5\frac{1}{2}$

$45°$

2

$\frac{1}{2}$ R

$3\frac{3}{4}$

$\frac{3}{8}$

$4\frac{1}{4}$

DOOR KNOCKER

1. Material: Cast aluminum or brass.

2. Finish: Polished (apply a coating of clear lacquer if the castings are of brass).

3. Initials (1/4 inch minimum height) may be etched, stamped or engraved on center band of the casting.

4. A 1/4 inch diameter rod threaded on both ends (1/4-20NC) is used to hold the unit to the door.

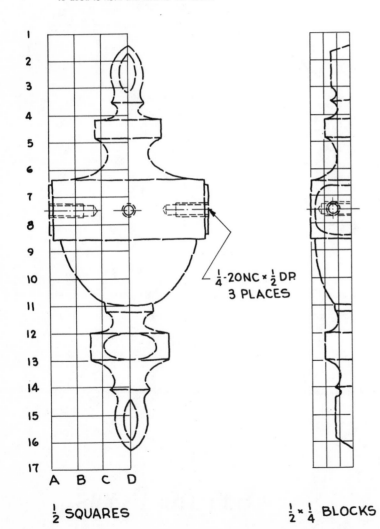

$\frac{1}{4}$-20NC × $\frac{1}{2}$ DP.
3 PLACES

$\frac{1}{2}$ SQUARES

$\frac{1}{2}$ × $\frac{1}{4}$ BLOCKS

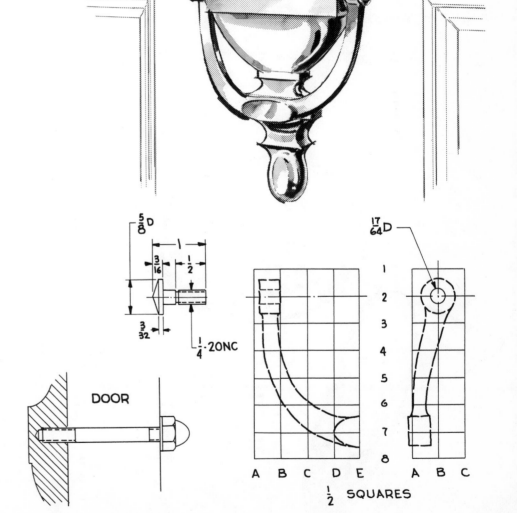

$\frac{5}{8}$ D

$\frac{3}{16}$ $\frac{1}{2}$

$\frac{3}{32}$

$\frac{1}{4}$-20NC

DOOR

$\frac{17}{64}$ D

$\frac{1}{2}$ SQUARES

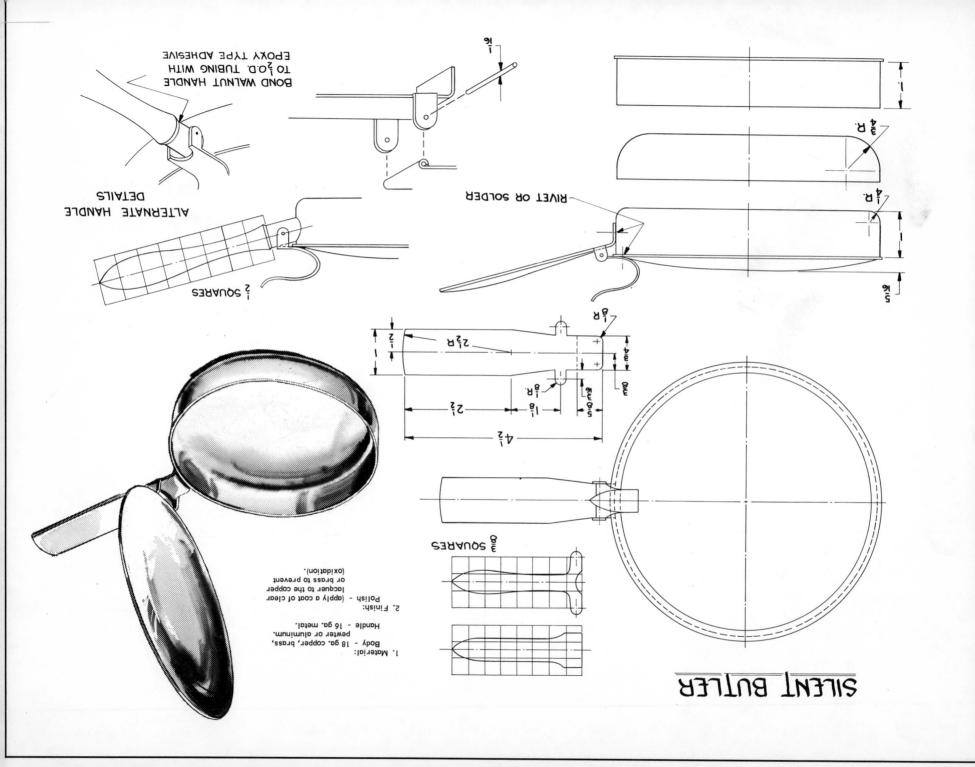

FIREPLACE GRATE

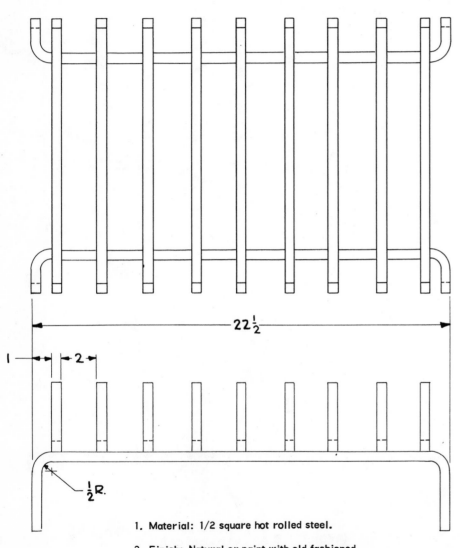

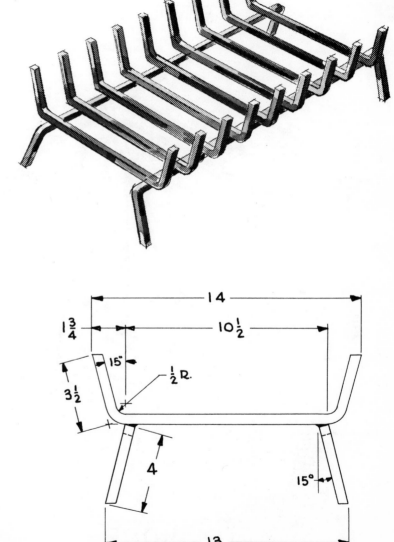

$22\frac{1}{2}$

1

2

$\frac{1}{2}$R.

14

$1\frac{3}{4}$

$10\frac{1}{2}$

15°

$\frac{1}{2}$R.

$3\frac{1}{2}$

4

15°

13

1. Material: 1/2 square hot rolled steel.

2. Finish: Natural or paint with old fashioned stove polish.

3. All weldments 1/8 or 3/16 fillet type.

BOOKEND

1. Material – 3/8 square or round brass, aluminum or hot rolled steel.

2. Finish – Brass can be polished or plated.
   Aluminum can be polished or painted flat black.
   Hot rolled steel can be painted flat black.

BRAZE JOINT OR DRILL
AND TAP FOR A #10-24NC
× $\frac{3}{4}$ LG. F.H. MACH. SCREW

DETAIL "A"

SEE DETAIL "A"

$\frac{3}{16}$

3

$1\frac{1}{2}$

$5\frac{1}{2}$

$2\frac{1}{2}$

$2\frac{1}{4}$

$\frac{3}{8}$ SQ.

$\frac{3}{4}$ R. (TYPICAL)

$\frac{3}{8}$ R. (TYPICAL)

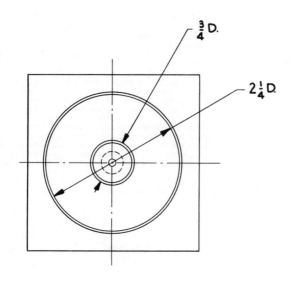

$\frac{3}{4}$ D.

$2\frac{1}{4}$ D.

BORED PEN BASE

1. Material: Aluminum, brass, stainless steel or C.F.S.

2. Finish: Satin finish or polished as desired.

3. Remove all burrs and sharp edges.

4. Cover base with felt.

5. Pen and pen holder secured from plastic supply firm or school shop supply vendor.

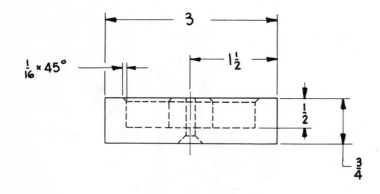

$\frac{1}{16} \times 45°$

3

$1\frac{1}{2}$

$\frac{1}{2}$

$\frac{3}{4}$

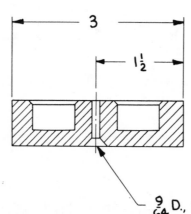

3

$1\frac{1}{2}$

$\frac{9}{64}$ D., C'SINK $\frac{3}{8}$ D × 82°

COMPRESSED AIR ENGINE

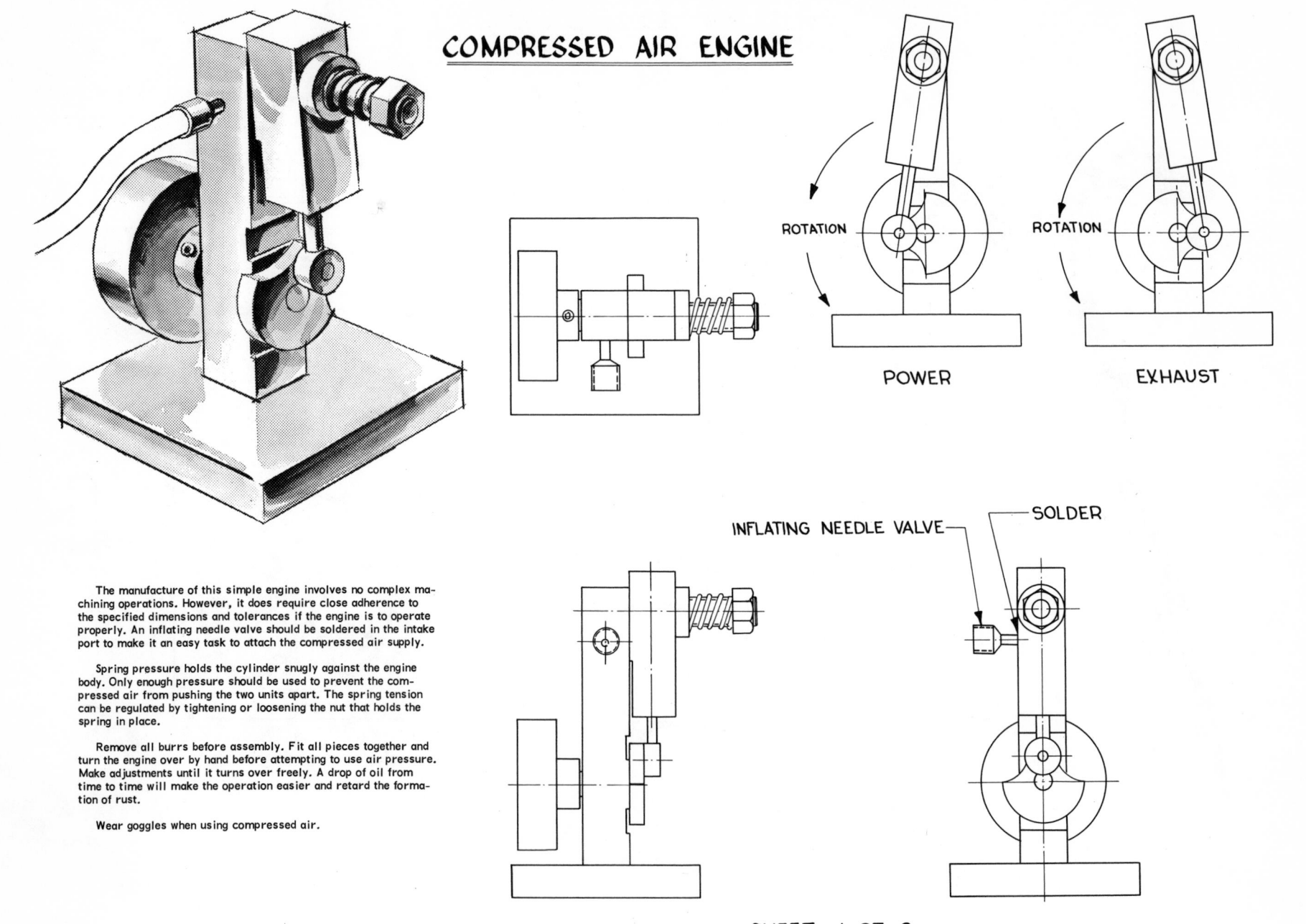

ROTATION

ROTATION

POWER

EXHAUST

INFLATING NEEDLE VALVE

SOLDER

The manufacture of this simple engine involves no complex machining operations. However, it does require close adherence to the specified dimensions and tolerances if the engine is to operate properly. An inflating needle valve should be soldered in the intake port to make it an easy task to attach the compressed air supply.

Spring pressure holds the cylinder snugly against the engine body. Only enough pressure should be used to prevent the compressed air from pushing the two units apart. The spring tension can be regulated by tightening or loosening the nut that holds the spring in place.

Remove all burrs before assembly. Fit all pieces together and turn the engine over by hand before attempting to use air pressure. Make adjustments until it turns over freely. A drop of oil from time to time will make the operation easier and retard the formation of rust.

Wear goggles when using compressed air.

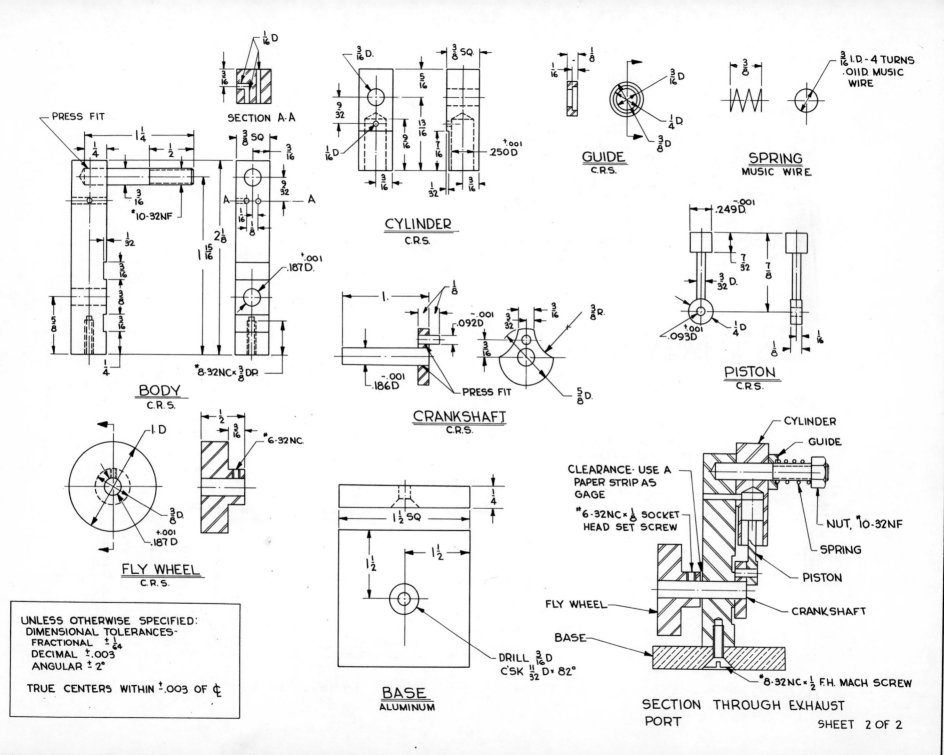

SECTION A·A

BODY
C.R.S.

CYLINDER
C.R.S.

GUIDE
C.R.S.

SPRING
MUSIC WIRE

PRESS FIT

#10-32NF

.187 D. +.001

#8·32NC × 3/8 DP.

CRANKSHAFT
C.R.S.

PRESS FIT

.186 D -.001

.092 D -.001

3/8 R.

5/8 D.

PISTON
C.R.S.

.249 D -.001

.093 D +.001

1/4 D.

3/32 D.

3/16 I.D.-4 TURNS
.011 D. MUSIC WIRE

FLY WHEEL
C.R.S.

I. D

#6-32NC.

3/8 D.

.187 D +.001

BASE
ALUMINUM

1 1/2 SQ.

DRILL 3/16 D
C'SK 11/32 D × 82°

CLEARANCE· USE A
PAPER STRIP AS
GAGE

#6·32NC × 1/8 SOCKET
HEAD SET SCREW

FLY WHEEL

BASE

CYLINDER

GUIDE

NUT, #10-32NF

SPRING

PISTON

CRANKSHAFT

#8·32NC × 1/2 F.H. MACH SCREW

SECTION THROUGH EXHAUST
PORT

SHEET 2 OF 2

UNLESS OTHERWISE SPECIFIED:
DIMENSIONAL TOLERANCES-
   FRACTIONAL ± 1/64
   DECIMAL ± .003
   ANGULAR ± 2°

TRUE CENTERS WITHIN ± .003 OF ₵

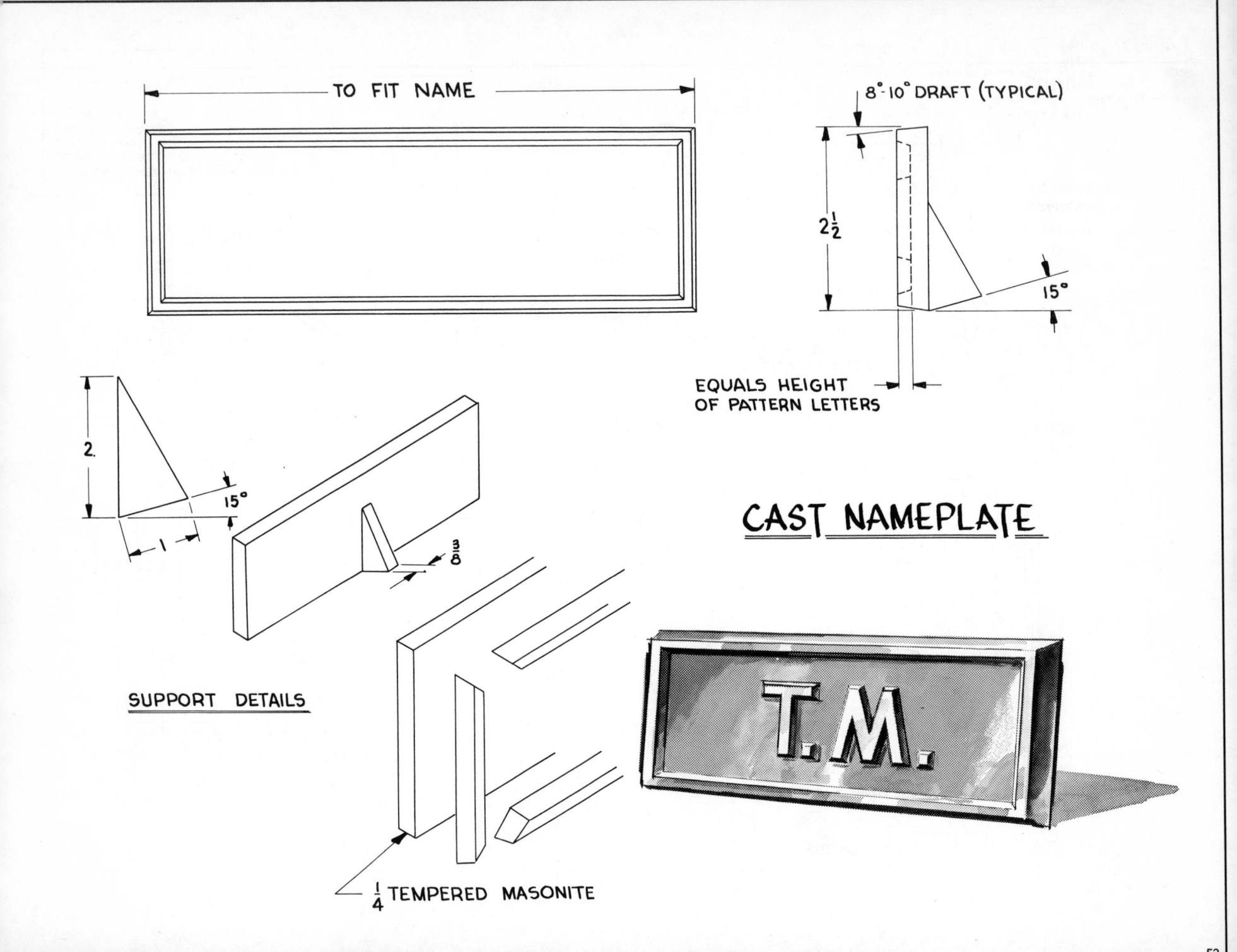

TO FIT NAME

8°-10° DRAFT (TYPICAL)

$2\frac{1}{2}$

15°

EQUALS HEIGHT
OF PATTERN LETTERS

2.

15°

1

$\frac{3}{8}$

CAST NAMEPLATE

SUPPORT DETAILS

$\frac{1}{4}$ TEMPERED MASONITE

SALAD SERVERS

1. Material: 1/8th half-hard aluminum.

2. Finish: Buff to a high polish or rub down with fine steel wool for a matt finish.

3. Taper ends before bending to shape.

4. Break all sharp edges.

5. If wood handles are used, treat them with a salad oil or finish them with DEFT.

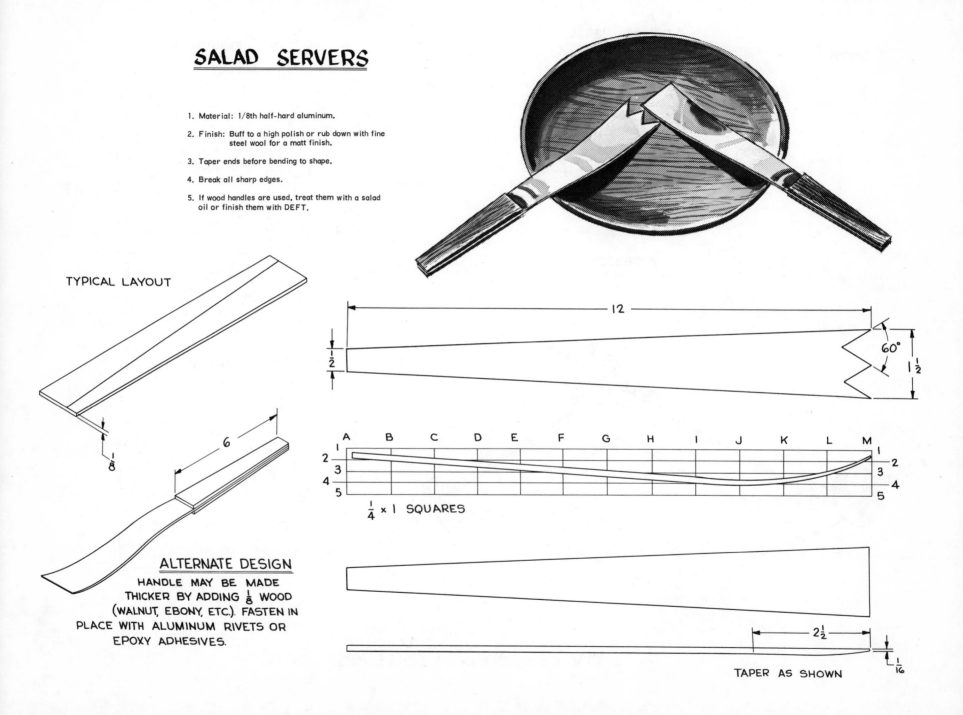

TYPICAL LAYOUT

12

$\frac{1}{2}$

60°

$1\frac{1}{2}$

$\frac{1}{8}$

6

| A | B | C | D | E | F | G | H | I | J | K | L | M |

$\frac{1}{4}$ x 1 SQUARES

ALTERNATE DESIGN
HANDLE MAY BE MADE THICKER BY ADDING $\frac{1}{8}$ WOOD (WALNUT, EBONY, ETC.). FASTEN IN PLACE WITH ALUMINUM RIVETS OR EPOXY ADHESIVES.

$2\frac{1}{2}$

$\frac{1}{16}$

TAPER AS SHOWN

PICTURE FRAME CLAMP

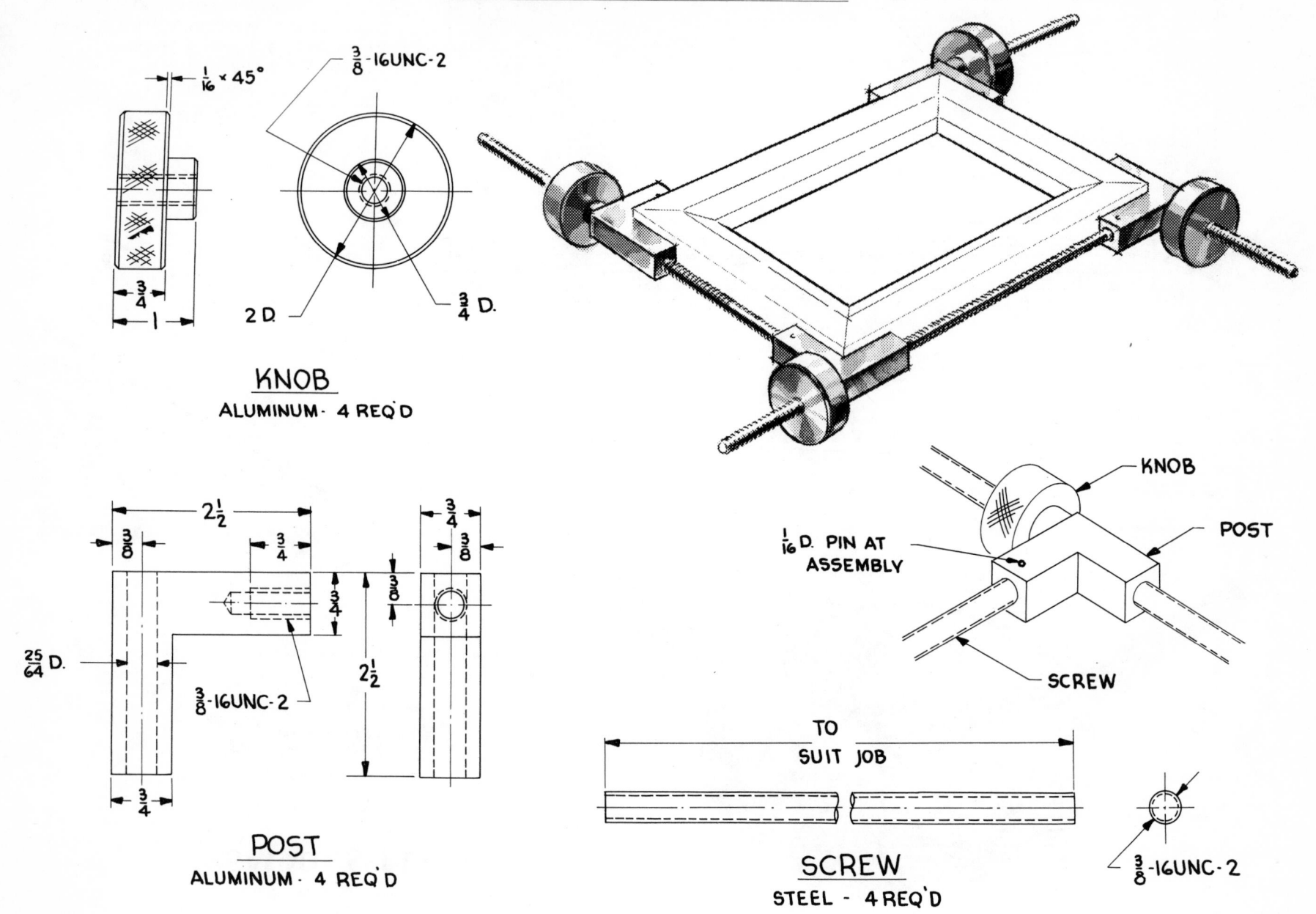

$\frac{1}{16} \times 45°$

$\frac{3}{8}$-16UNC-2

2 D.

$\frac{3}{4}$ D.

$\frac{3}{4}$

1

KNOB
ALUMINUM · 4 REQ'D

$2\frac{1}{2}$

$\frac{3}{8}$

$\frac{3}{4}$

$\frac{3}{4}$

$\frac{3}{8}$ $\frac{3}{8}$

$\frac{3}{4}$

$\frac{3}{8}$

$2\frac{1}{2}$

$\frac{25}{64}$ D.

$\frac{3}{8}$-16UNC-2

$\frac{3}{4}$

POST
ALUMINUM · 4 REQ'D

KNOB

POST

$\frac{1}{16}$ D. PIN AT ASSEMBLY

SCREW

TO SUIT JOB

$\frac{3}{8}$-16UNC-2

SCREW
STEEL - 4 REQ'D

CAST BOOKENDS

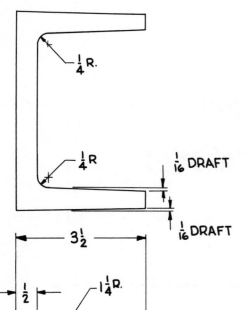

$\frac{1}{4}$ R.

$\frac{1}{4}$ R

$\frac{1}{16}$ DRAFT

$\frac{1}{16}$ DRAFT

1. Material: Cast aluminum or brass.

2. Finish: Polished or matt surface.

3. Two bookends required.

4. Allow 1/16 draft on bottom (see sketch of pattern) for easy removal from sand. Finish bottom 90 deg. to back.

5. Round all sharp edges.

6. Cement felt or cork to bottom.

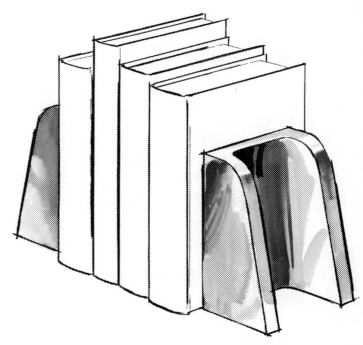

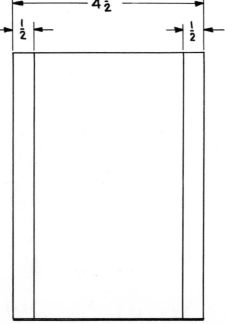

$3\frac{1}{2}$

$\frac{1}{2}$

$1\frac{1}{4}$ R.

$1\frac{1}{4}$

6

$4\frac{1}{2}$

$\frac{1}{2}$

$\frac{1}{2}$

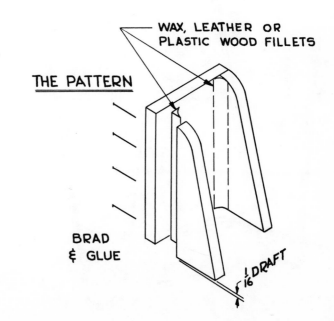

WAX, LEATHER OR PLASTIC WOOD FILLETS

THE PATTERN

BRAD & GLUE

$\frac{1}{16}$ DRAFT

STACKING
PATIO TABLES

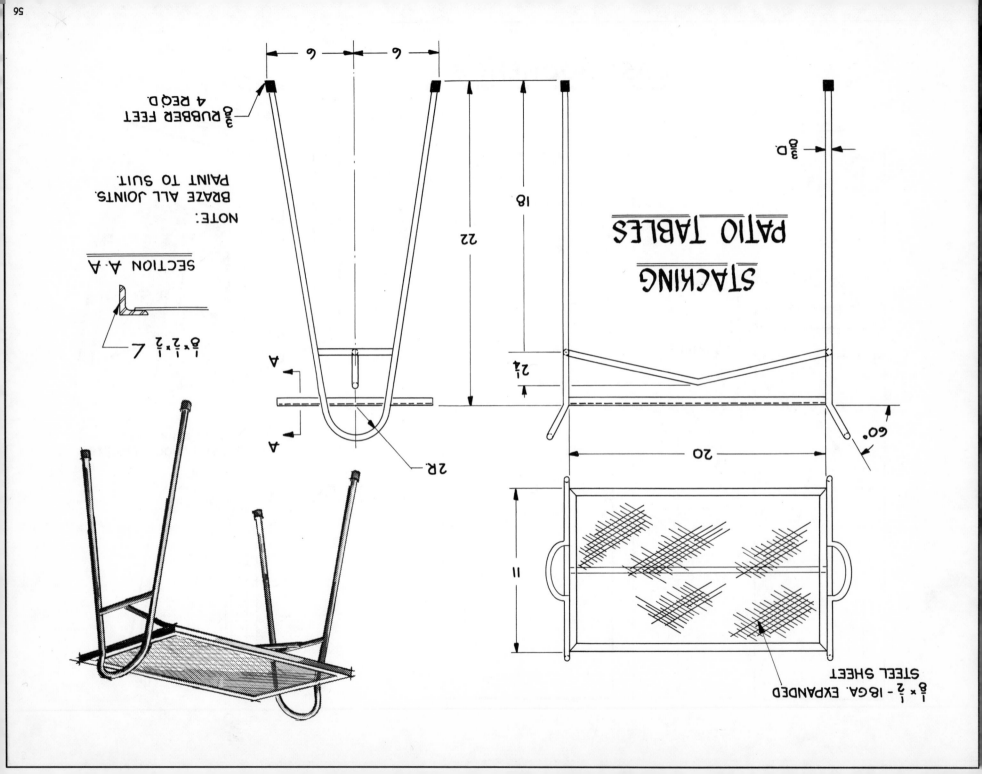

RUBBER FEET
4 REQ'D.

NOTE:
BRAZE ALL JOINTS.
PAINT TO SUIT.

SECTION A·A

$\frac{1}{8} \times 2 \times \frac{1}{2}$

2R

A

A

6

6

18

22

2$\frac{1}{4}$

60°

20

11

$\frac{1}{8} \times \frac{1}{2}$ - 18 GA. EXPANDED
STEEL SHEET

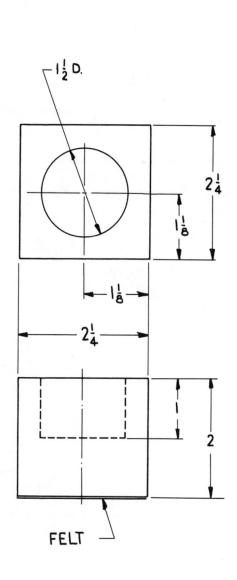

$1\frac{1}{2}$ D.

$2\frac{1}{4}$

$1\frac{1}{8}$

$1\frac{1}{8}$

$2\frac{1}{4}$

2

FELT

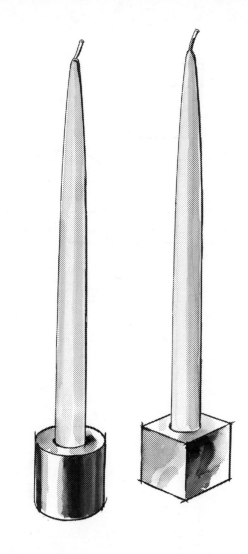

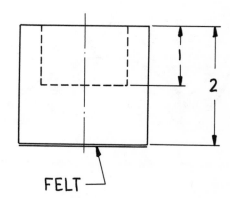

$1\frac{1}{2}$ D

$2\frac{1}{4}$ D.

2

FELT

CANDLE HOLDERS

1. Material: Aluminum or brass.

2. Finish: Polished or matte.

3. Break all sharp edges.

4. Cement felt to base to protect surface
   on which candle holder is placed.

METAL SCULPTURE

BASE 1½ × 8 × ½

EPOXY INTO BASE

FELT

This is an IDEA project. Use your imagination in planning how to make and use this project – bookends, paperweights, etc. What materials to use – 1/8 brass, copper, aluminum, pewter for the body, or form it from 1/8 dia. brazing rod and hard solder it together? Use the brazing rod for legs. The base may be made from hardwood, metal, plastic, slate, marble, glass, etc.

Think of the many animal, aquatic and plant forms that may be adapted.

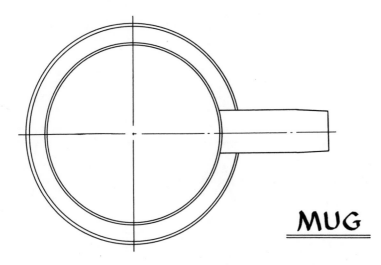

MUG

1. Material: Copper, brass or pewter 16-18 ga.

2. Finish: Exterior polished, interior matt or satin finish. The entire mug or just the interior may be silver plated.

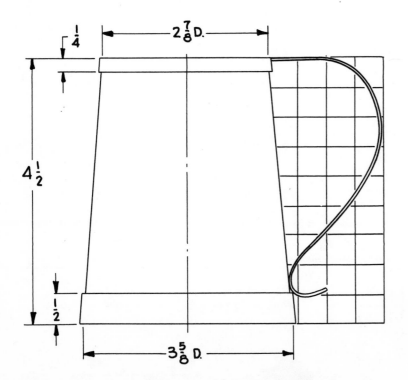

$\frac{1}{4}$

$2\frac{7}{8}$ D.

$4\frac{1}{2}$

$\frac{1}{2}$

$3\frac{5}{8}$ D.

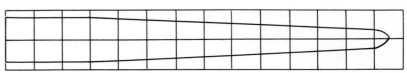

$\frac{1}{2}$ SQUARES

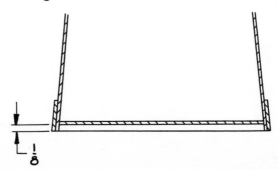

$\frac{1}{8}$

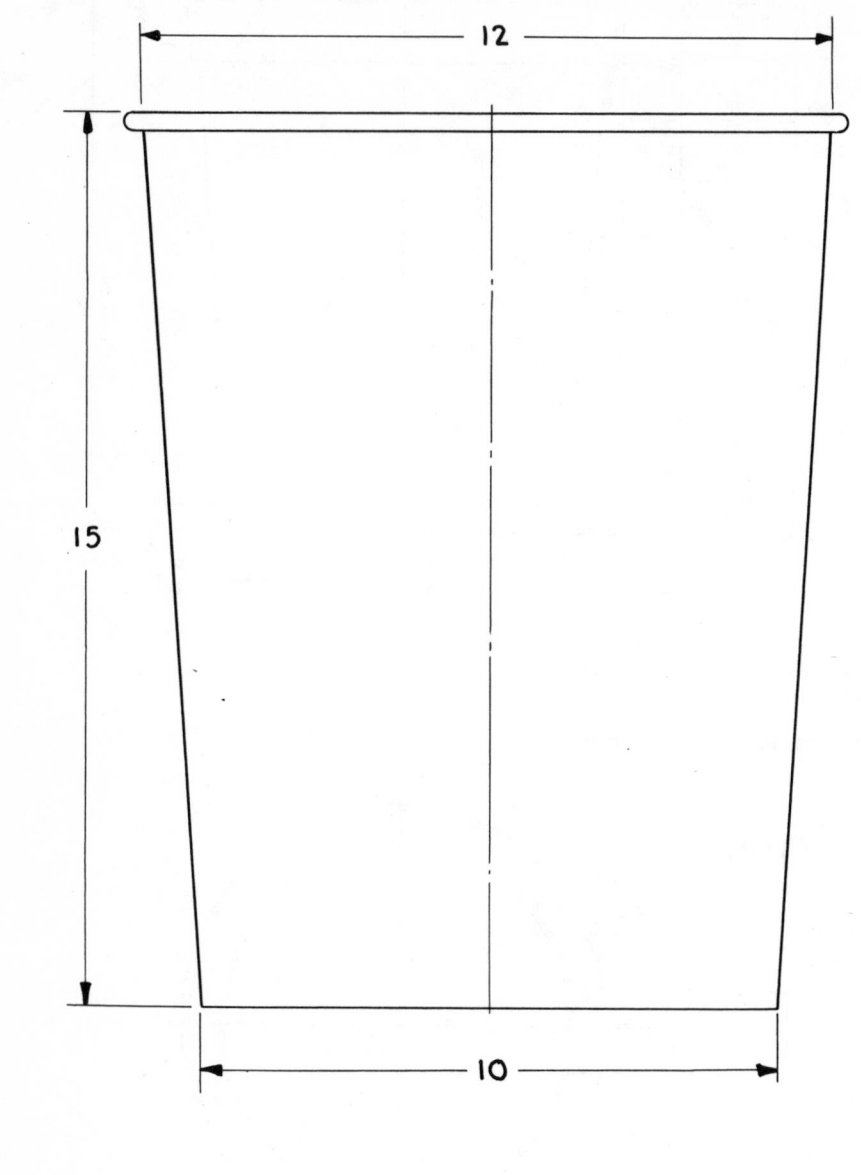

12

15

10

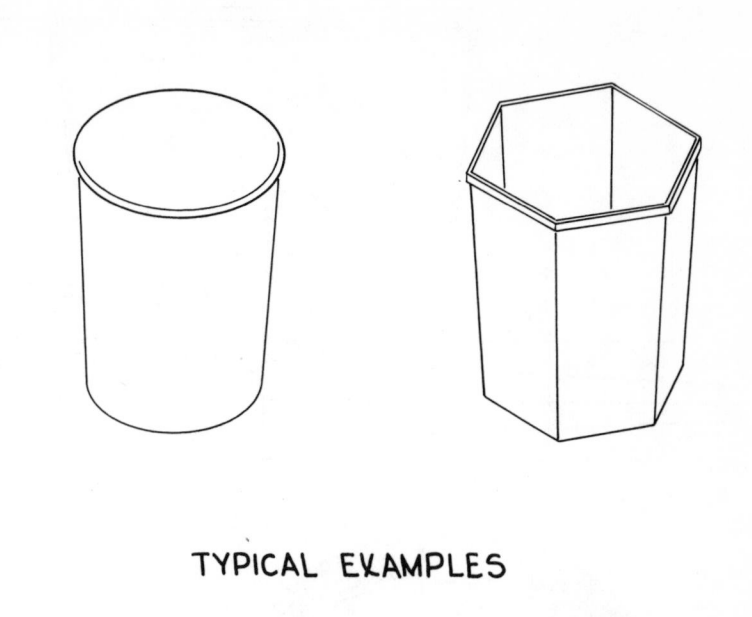

TYPICAL EXAMPLES

WASTE BASKET DESIGN PROBLEM

Design, develop the patterns and manufacture a wastebasket using the basic dimensions shown in the drawing. Use accepted sheet metal practices to assemble the unit. Sheet material (28 ga.) may be brass, copper, tin or aluminum. Aluminum sheet is available in a variety of embossed and perforated patterns at most hardware stores.

Spot welding may be substituted for soldering.

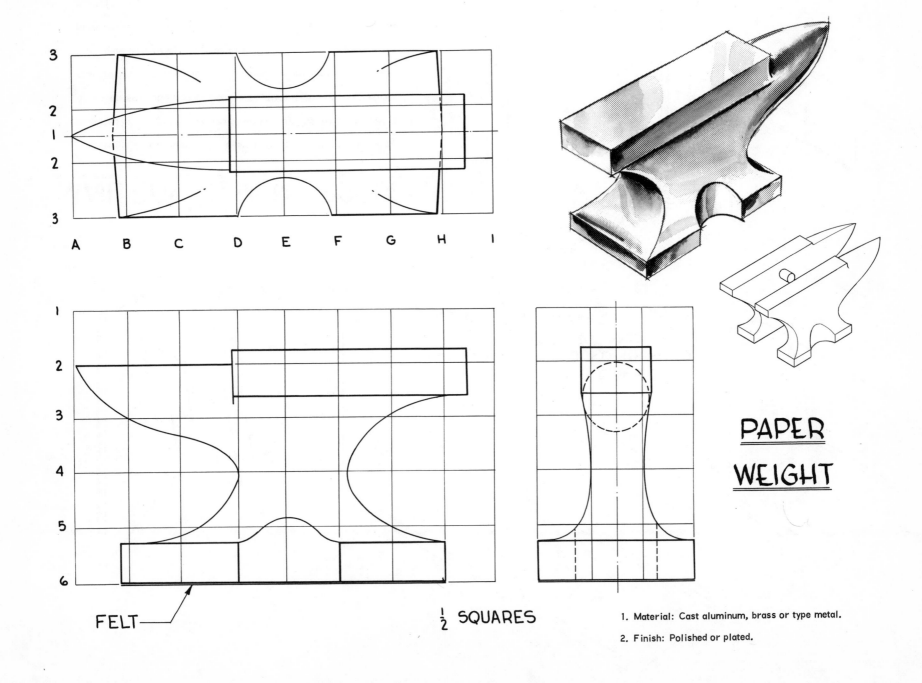

FELT

$\frac{1}{2}$ SQUARES

PAPER

WEIGHT

1. Material: Cast aluminum, brass or type metal.

2. Finish: Polished or plated.

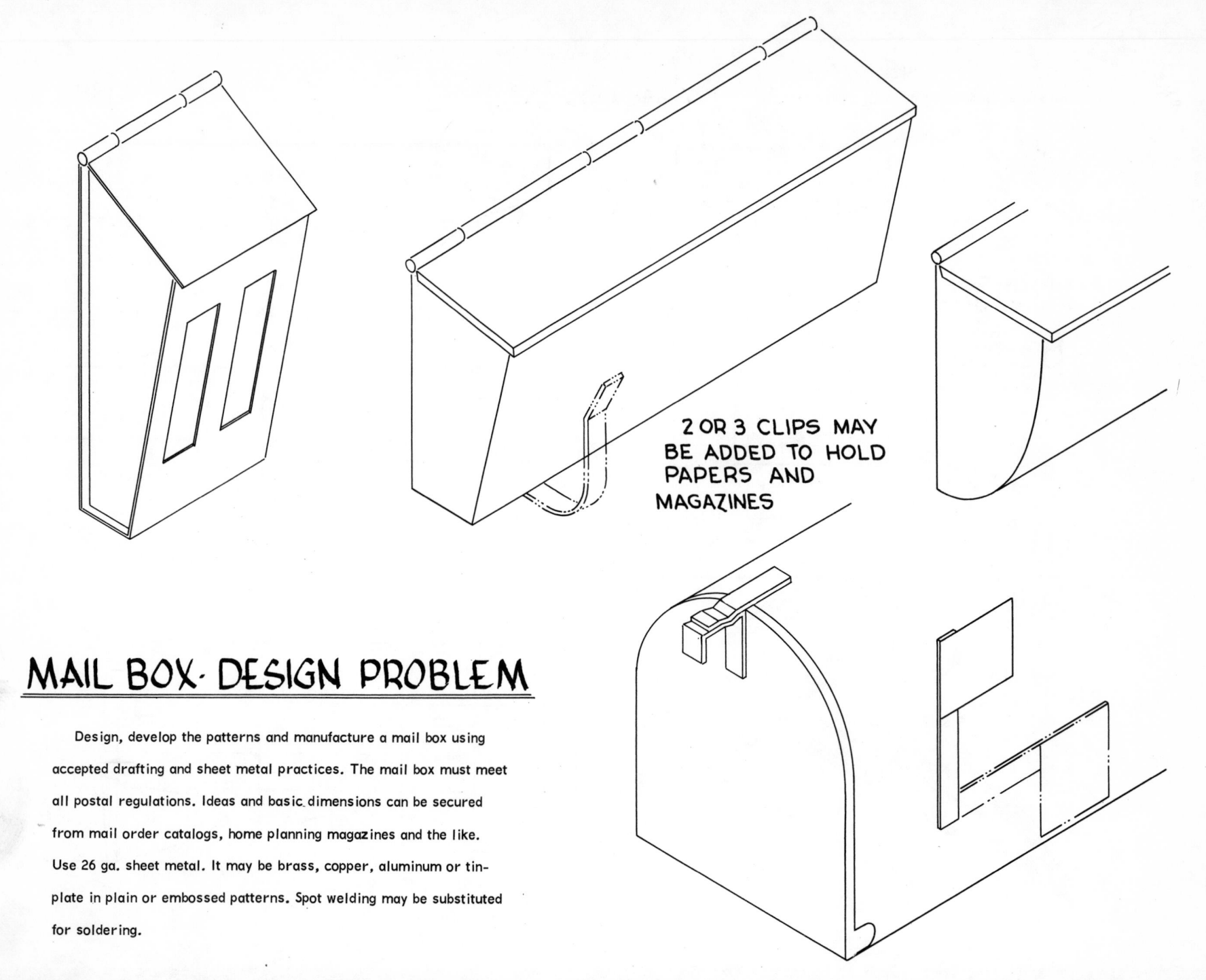

2 OR 3 CLIPS MAY
BE ADDED TO HOLD
PAPERS AND
MAGAZINES

MAIL BOX· DESIGN PROBLEM

Design, develop the patterns and manufacture a mail box using

accepted drafting and sheet metal practices. The mail box must meet

all postal regulations. Ideas and basic dimensions can be secured

from mail order catalogs, home planning magazines and the like.

Use 26 ga. sheet metal. It may be brass, copper, aluminum or tin-

plate in plain or embossed patterns. Spot welding may be substituted

for soldering.

GRAVITY CENTER PUNCH

1. Material: As noted.

2. Finish: Accepted machine shop practice – little or no filing.

3. Tolerances: As indicated by your instructor.

4. Break all sharp edges.

5. Heat treat only the point section of the punch.

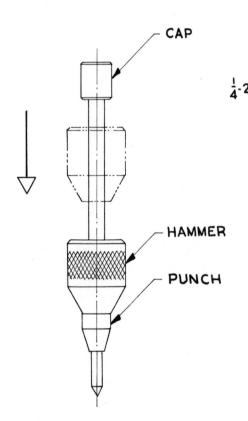

CAP

HAMMER

PUNCH

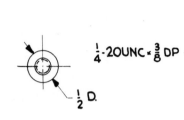

$\frac{1}{4}$-20UNC × $\frac{3}{8}$ DP

$\frac{1}{2}$ D.

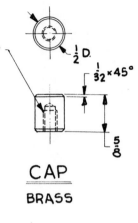

$\frac{1}{2}$ D.

$\frac{1}{32}$×45°

$\frac{5}{8}$

CAP

BRASS

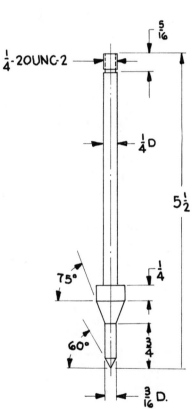

$\frac{1}{4}$-20UNC-2

$\frac{5}{16}$

$\frac{1}{4}$ D

$5\frac{1}{2}$

75°

60°

$\frac{1}{4}$

$3\frac{3}{4}$

$\frac{3}{16}$ D.

PUNCH

DRILL ROD - HEAT TREAT

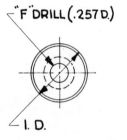

"F" DRILL (.257 D.)

I. D.

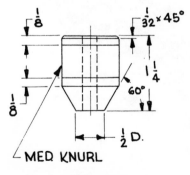

$\frac{1}{8}$

$\frac{1}{32}$×45°

$1\frac{1}{4}$

$\frac{1}{8}$

60°

$\frac{1}{2}$ D.

MED KNURL

HAMMER

C.R.S.

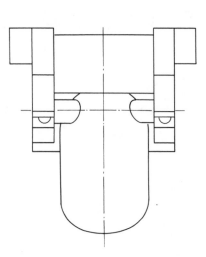

The idea for this mortar was taken from a model of a proposed Civil War mortar. It is interesting to note that models were used instead of blueprints during this period because so few of the workers were capable of understanding the lines, symbols and notations found on the print.

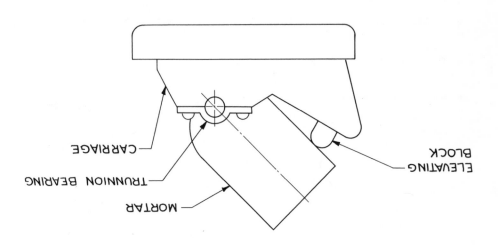

TRUNNION BEARING

CARRIAGE

ELEVATING BLOCK

MORTAR

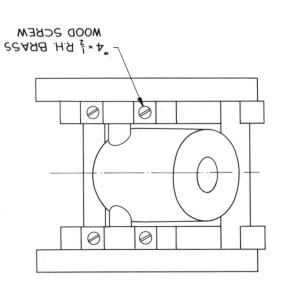

"4 x ½ R.H. BRASS WOOD SCREW

CIVIL WAR MORTAR

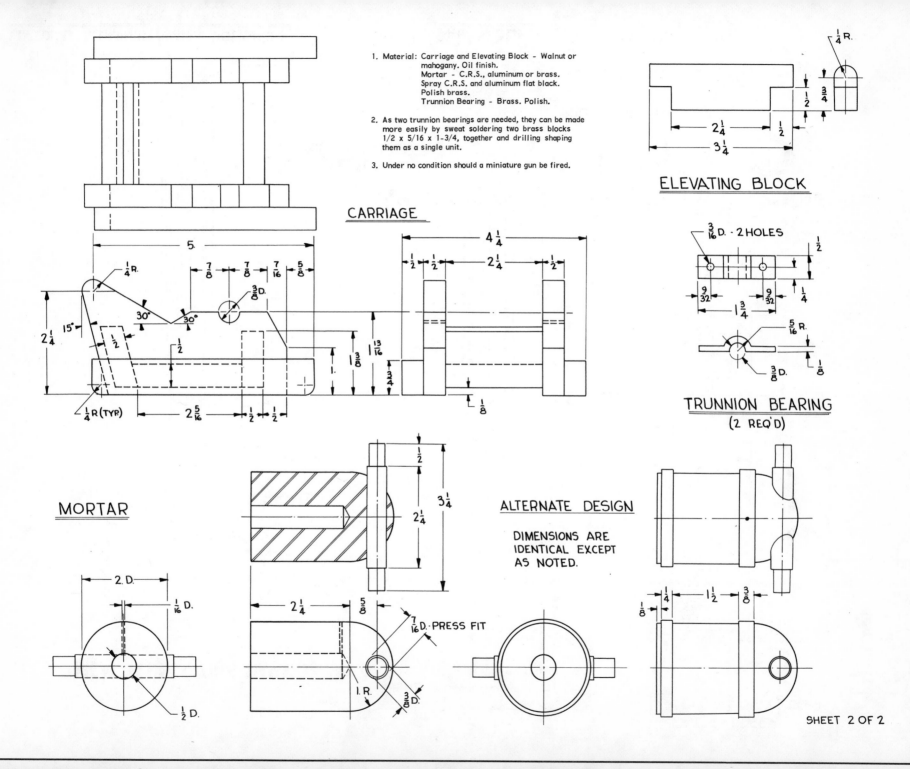

1. Material: Carriage and Elevating Block - Walnut or
   mahogany. Oil finish.
   Mortar - C.R.S., aluminum or brass.
   Spray C.R.S. and aluminum flat black.
   Polish brass.
   Trunnion Bearing - Brass. Polish.

2. As two trunnion bearings are needed, they can be made
   more easily by sweat soldering two brass blocks
   1/2 x 5/16 x 1-3/4, together and drilling shaping
   them as a single unit.

3. Under no condition should a miniature gun be fired.

ELEVATING BLOCK

CARRIAGE

TRUNNION BEARING
(2 REQ'D)

MORTAR

ALTERNATE DESIGN

DIMENSIONS ARE
IDENTICAL EXCEPT
AS NOTED.

SHEET 2 OF 2

65

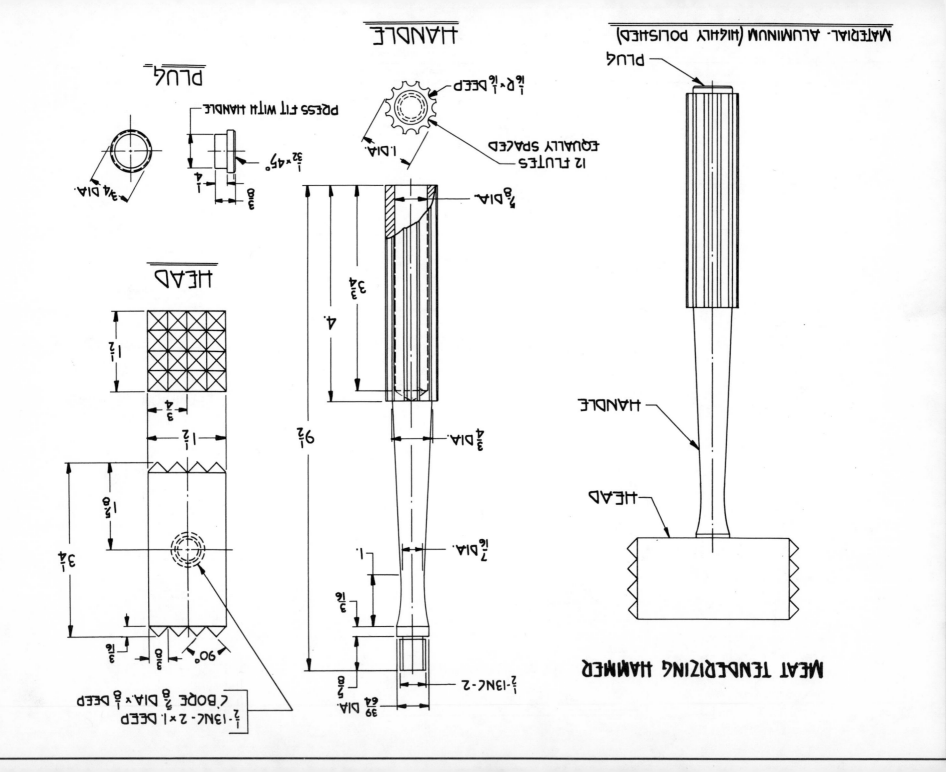

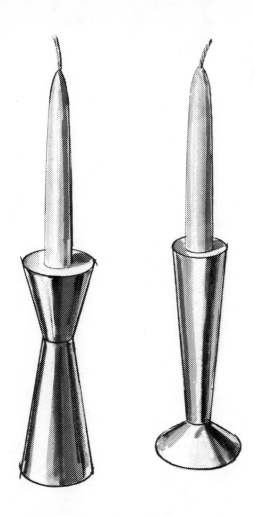

CONTEMPORARY
CANDLESTICKS

1. Material - Aluminum or brass.

2. Finish - Highly polished or matt surface.

3. Candlesticks may be made in two parts and screwed together.

4. Cover base with felt or cork.

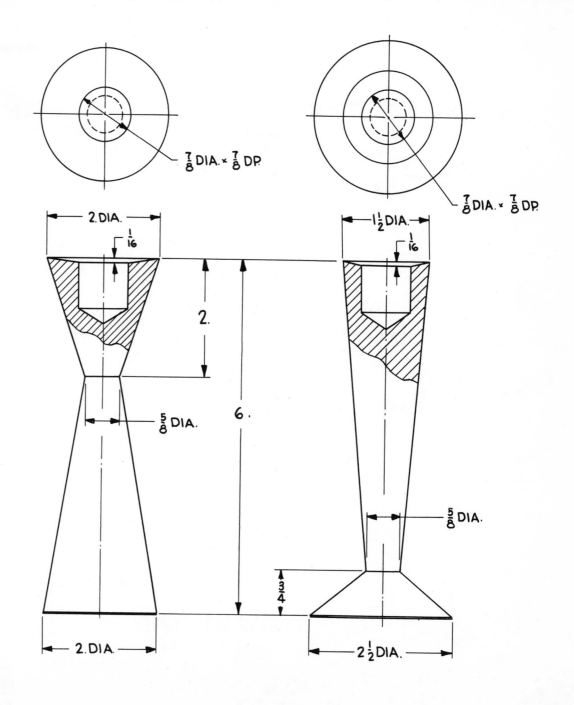

$\frac{7}{8}$ DIA. × $\frac{7}{8}$ DP.

$\frac{7}{8}$ DIA. × $\frac{7}{8}$ DP.

2. DIA.

1$\frac{1}{2}$ DIA.

$\frac{1}{16}$

$\frac{1}{16}$

2.

6.

$\frac{5}{8}$ DIA.

$\frac{5}{8}$ DIA.

$\frac{3}{4}$

2. DIA.

2$\frac{1}{2}$ DIA.

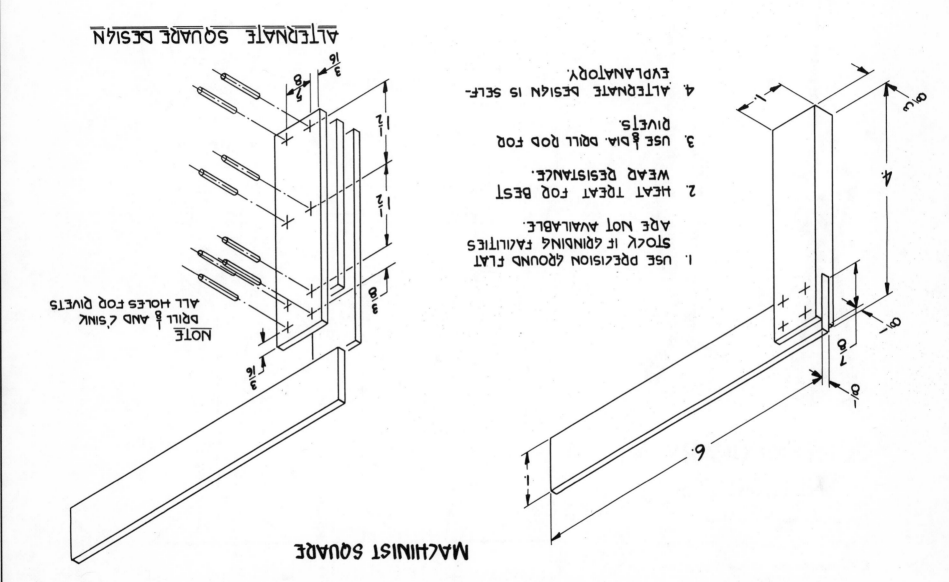

ALTERNATE SQUARE DESIGN

NOTE
DRILL $\frac{1}{8}$ AND C'SINK
ALL HOLES FOR RIVETS

$\frac{3}{16}$

$\frac{5}{8}$

$1\frac{1}{2}$

$1\frac{1}{2}$

$3\frac{3}{8}$

$\frac{3}{16}$

4. ALTERNATE DESIGN IS SELF-
   EXPLANATORY.

3. USE $\frac{3}{8}$ DIA. DRILL ROD FOR
   RIVETS.

2. HEAT TREAT FOR BEST
   WEAR RESISTANCE.

1. USE PRECISION GROUND FLAT
   STOCK IF GRINDING FACILITIES
   ARE NOT AVAILABLE.

1

$\frac{3}{16}$

4

$\frac{7}{8}$

$\frac{1}{16}$

$\frac{3}{16}$

6.

1

MACHINIST SQUARE

FORGED ANDIRON

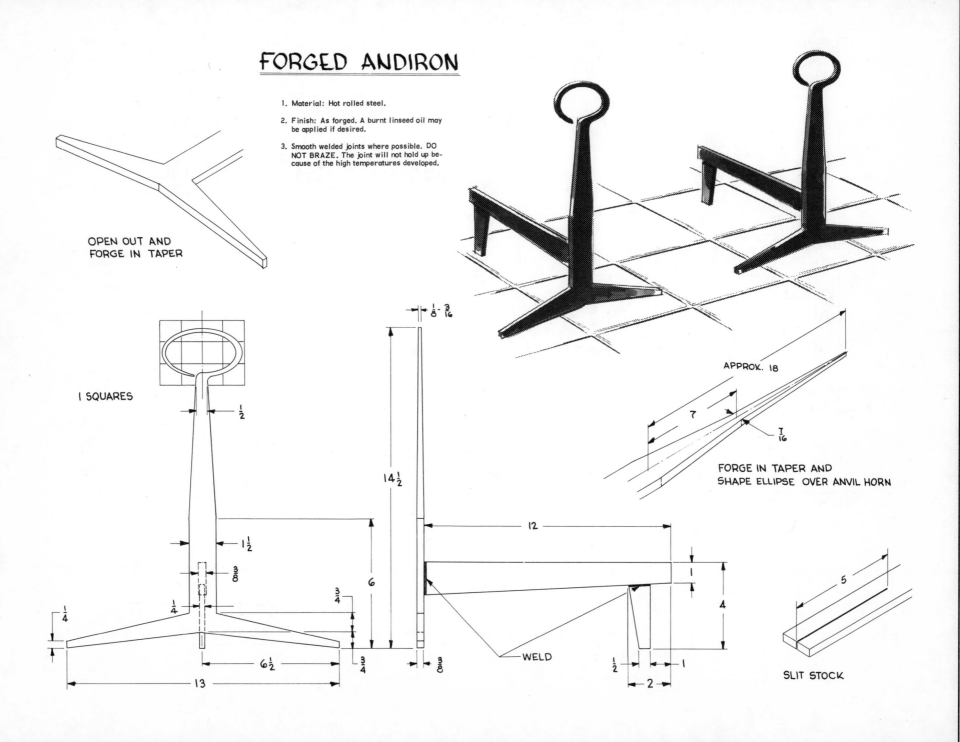

1. Material: Hot rolled steel.

2. Finish: As forged. A burnt linseed oil may be applied if desired.

3. Smooth welded joints where possible. DO NOT BRAZE. The joint will not hold up because of the high temperatures developed.

OPEN OUT AND FORGE IN TAPER

1 SQUARES

$\frac{1}{2}$

$1\frac{1}{2}$

$\frac{3}{8}$

$\frac{1}{4}$

$\frac{1}{4}$

$6\frac{1}{2}$

13

$14\frac{1}{2}$

6

$\frac{3}{4}$

$\frac{3}{4}$

$\frac{3}{8}$

$\frac{1}{8}$ · $\frac{3}{16}$

12

WELD

$\frac{1}{2}$

2

1

1

4

APPROX. 18

7

$\frac{7}{16}$

FORGE IN TAPER AND SHAPE ELLIPSE OVER ANVIL HORN

5

SLIT STOCK

14 TO 22

4

$1\frac{3}{8}$

$\frac{1}{2}$ SQUARES

COLONIAL STRAP HINGE

1. Material: Hot rolled steel.

2. Finish: As forged – may be painted flat black.

3. Mount pintle and hinge with 3/16 – 1/4 lag bolts.

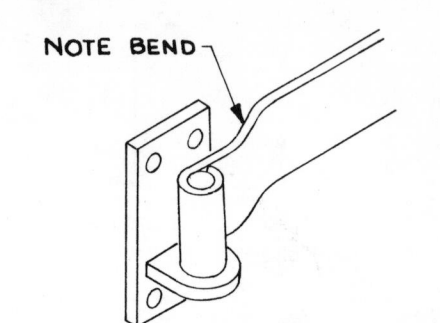

NOTE BEND

PINTLE & HINGE DETAIL

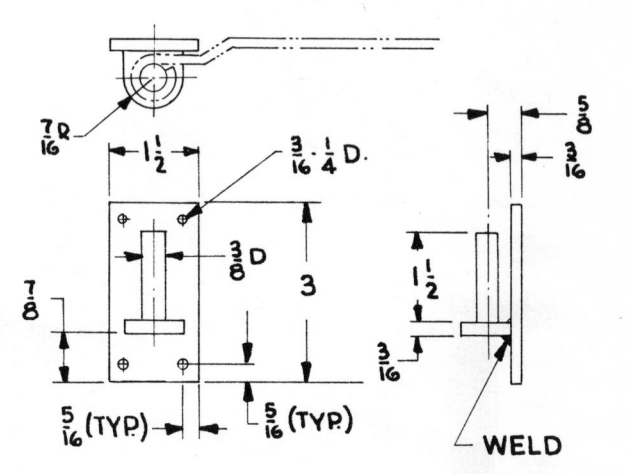

$\frac{7}{16}$ R

$1\frac{1}{2}$

$\frac{3}{16} \cdot \frac{1}{4}$ D.

$\frac{3}{8}$ D

3

$\frac{7}{8}$

$\frac{5}{16}$ (TYP.)

$\frac{5}{16}$ (TYP.)

$\frac{5}{8}$

$\frac{3}{16}$

$1\frac{1}{2}$

$\frac{3}{16}$

WELD

PINTLE

PLANISHED **NOT** PEENED

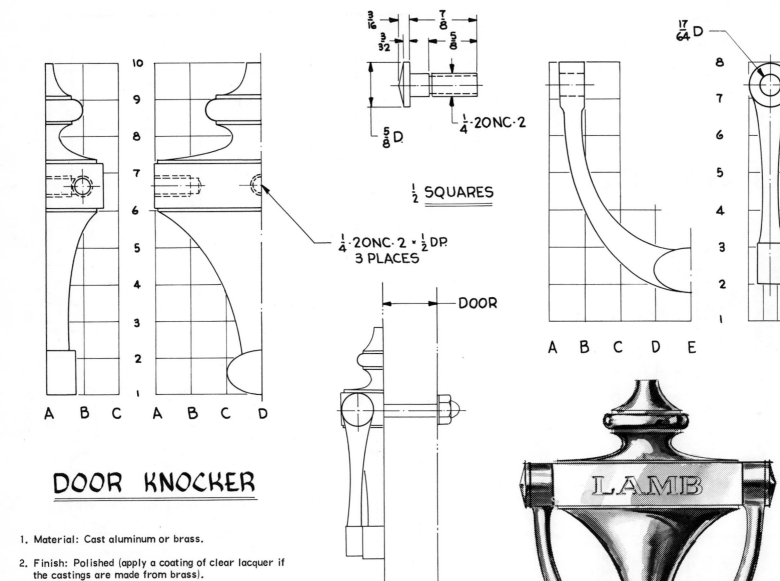

$\frac{1}{2}$ SQUARES

$\frac{1}{4}$·20NC·2 × $\frac{1}{2}$DP.
3 PLACES

$\frac{1}{4}$·20NC·2

$\frac{5}{8}$ D.

$\frac{17}{64}$ D

$\frac{1}{2}$ × $\frac{5}{16}$ GRID

DOOR

DOOR KNOCKER

1. Material: Cast aluminum or brass.

2. Finish: Polished (apply a coating of clear lacquer if the castings are made from brass).

3. Initials or name (1/4 inch minimum height) may be etched, stamped or engraved on center band of the casting.

4. A 1/4 inch diameter rod threaded on both ends (1/4-20NC) is used to hold the unit to the door.

LAMB

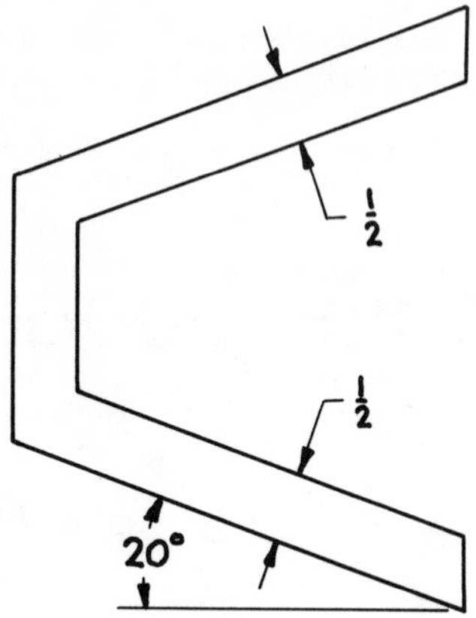

$\frac{1}{16}$ DRAFT

$\frac{1}{2}$

$\frac{1}{2}$

20°

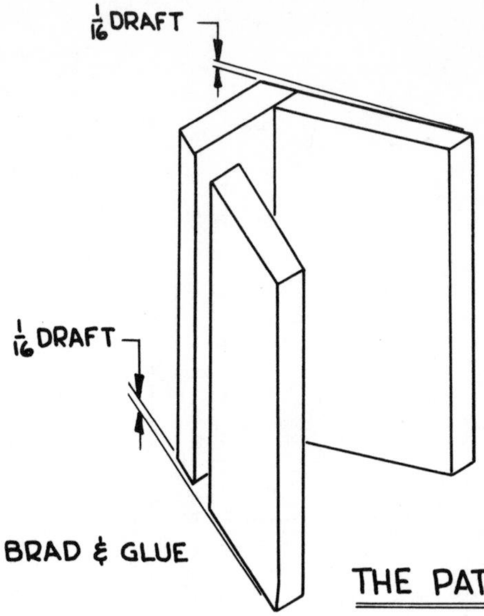

$\frac{1}{16}$ DRAFT

BRAD & GLUE

THE PATTERN

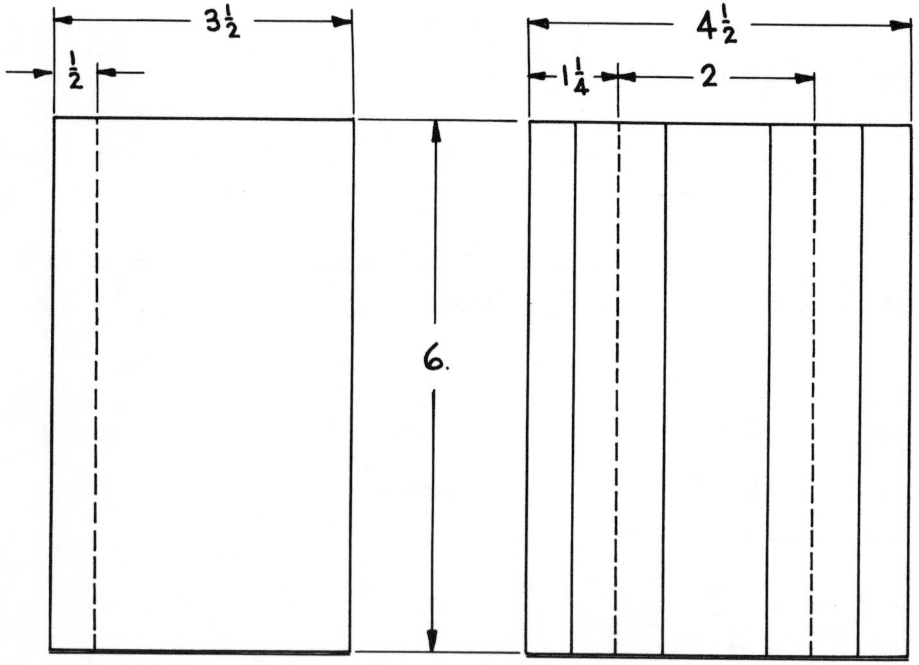

$3\frac{1}{2}$

$\frac{1}{2}$

$4\frac{1}{2}$

$1\frac{1}{4}$

2

6.

CAST BOOKENDS

1. Material: Cast aluminum or brass.

2. Finish: Polished or matt surface.

3. Two bookends required.

4. Allow 1/16 draft on bottom and top (see sketch of pattern) for easy removal from sand. Finish bottom and top 90 deg. to back.

5. Round all sharp edges.

6. Cement cork or felt on bottom.

PATIO SERVING CART

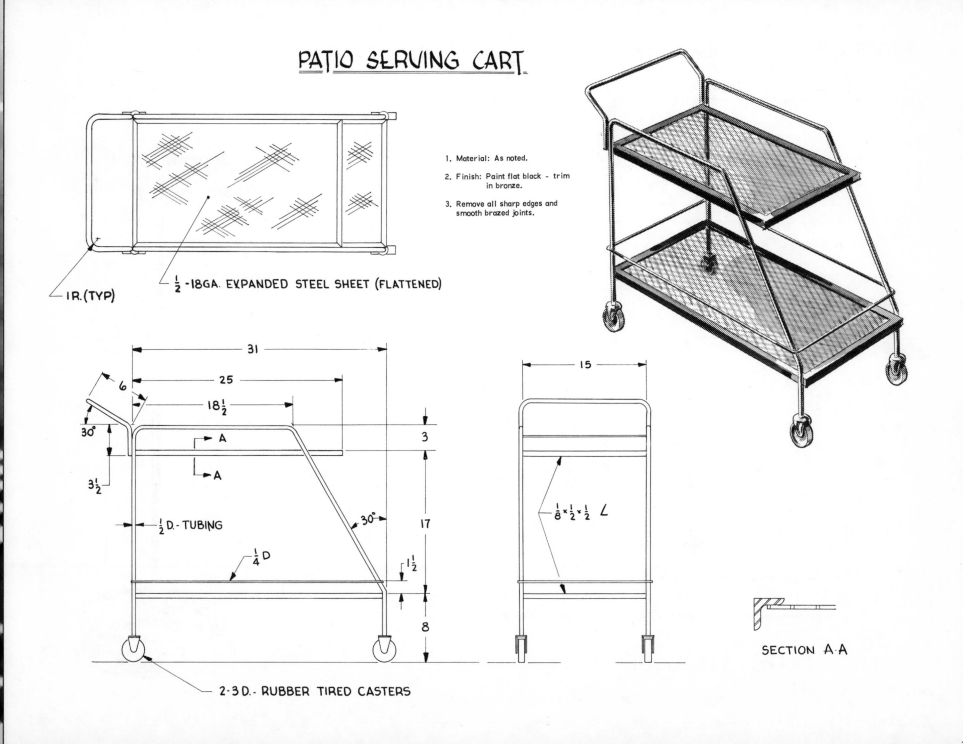

½ -18GA. EXPANDED STEEL SHEET (FLATTENED)

IR.(TYP)

1. Material: As noted.

2. Finish: Paint flat black – trim in bronze.

3. Remove all sharp edges and smooth brazed joints.

31

25

18½

6

30°

3½

½ D.- TUBING

¼ D

30°

A

A

3

17

1½

8

15

⅛ × ½ × ½ L

SECTION A·A

2-3 D.- RUBBER TIRED CASTERS

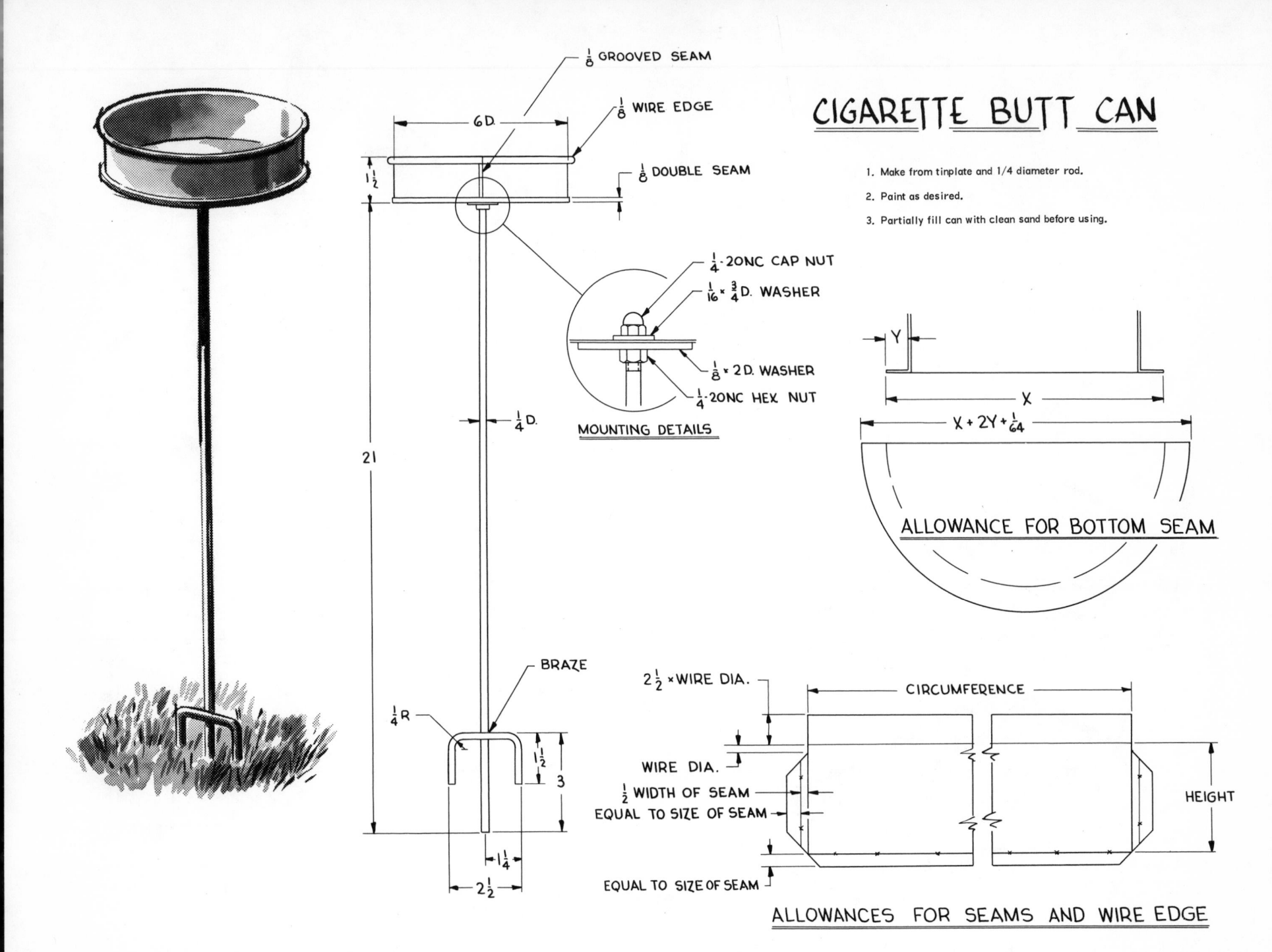

CIGARETTE BUTT CAN

$\frac{1}{8}$ GROOVED SEAM

$\frac{1}{8}$ WIRE EDGE

$\frac{1}{8}$ DOUBLE SEAM

1. Make from tinplate and 1/4 diameter rod.

2. Paint as desired.

3. Partially fill can with clean sand before using.

6 D.

$1\frac{1}{2}$

$\frac{1}{4}$ D.

21

$\frac{1}{4}$-20NC CAP NUT

$\frac{1}{16} \times \frac{3}{4}$ D. WASHER

$\frac{1}{8} \times 2$ D. WASHER

$\frac{1}{4}$-20NC HEX NUT

MOUNTING DETAILS

Y

X

$X + 2Y + \frac{1}{64}$

ALLOWANCE FOR BOTTOM SEAM

BRAZE

$\frac{1}{4}$ R

$1\frac{1}{2}$

3

$1\frac{1}{4}$

$2\frac{1}{2}$

$2\frac{1}{2}$ × WIRE DIA.

WIRE DIA.

$\frac{1}{2}$ WIDTH OF SEAM

EQUAL TO SIZE OF SEAM

EQUAL TO SIZE OF SEAM

CIRCUMFERENCE

HEIGHT

ALLOWANCES FOR SEAMS AND WIRE EDGE

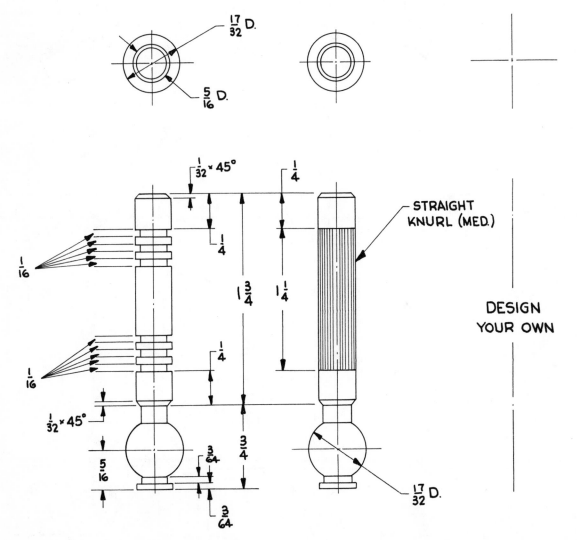

$\frac{17}{32}$ D.

$\frac{5}{16}$ D.

$\frac{1}{32} \times 45°$

$\frac{1}{4}$

$\frac{1}{16}$

$\frac{1}{16}$

$\frac{1}{4}$

$\frac{1}{4}$

$1\frac{3}{4}$

$1\frac{1}{4}$

$\frac{1}{4}$

$\frac{1}{32} \times 45°$

$\frac{5}{16}$

$\frac{3}{64}$

$\frac{3}{4}$

$\frac{3}{64}$

STRAIGHT
KNURL (MED.)

$\frac{17}{32}$ D.

DESIGN
YOUR OWN

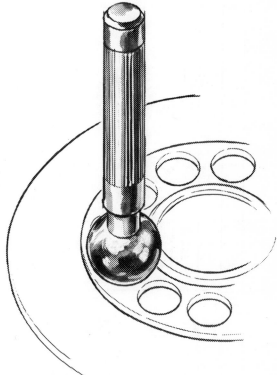

PHONE
FINGER

1. Material: Aluminum, brass, stainless steel.

2. Finish: As machined.

3. When designing your own, it is best to make a wooden model to see whether it will work properly without marring the figures on the number dial.

92

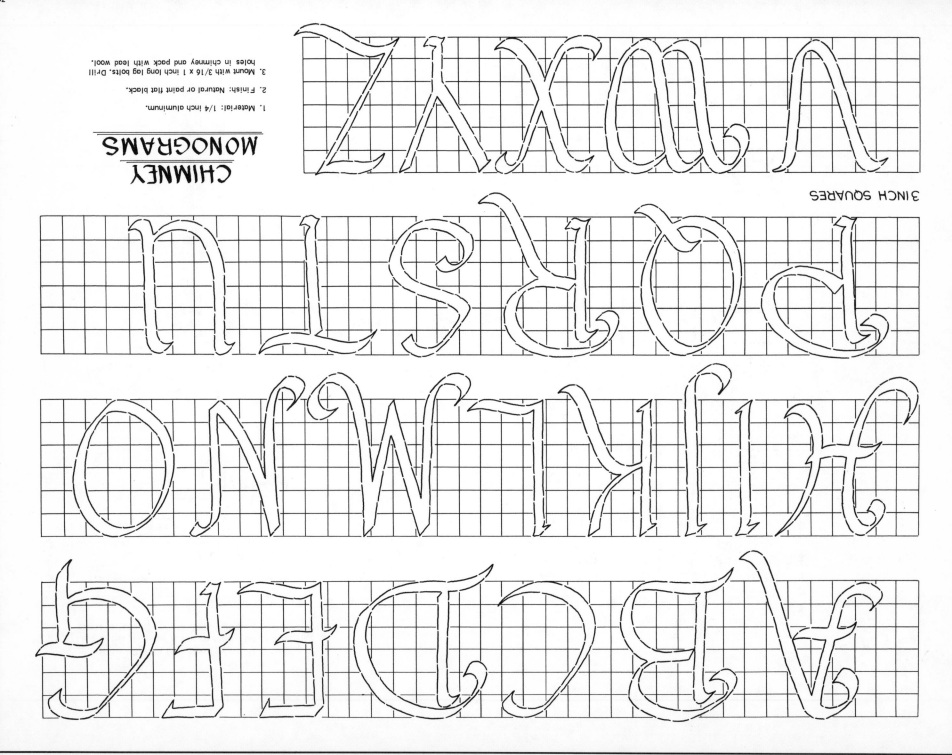

CHIMNEY MONOGRAMS

1. Material: 1/4 inch aluminum.
2. Finish: Natural or paint flat black.
3. Mount with 3/16 x 1 inch long lag bolts. Drill holes in chimney and pack with lead wool.

3 INCH SQUARES

CHILD'S CHALK BOARD

1. Material: Frame - as noted.
   Board - 1/8 tempered hardboard.

2. Finish: Frame - natural.
   Board - coat with chalk board paint (green).

3. Mount with screws or bolts.

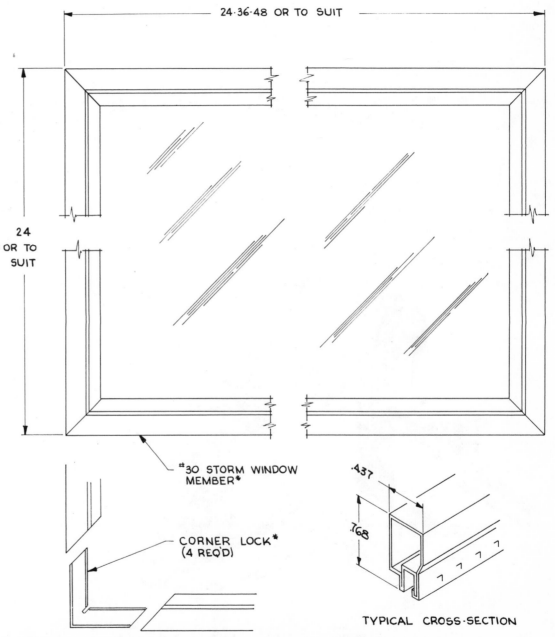

24·36·48 OR TO SUIT

24 OR TO SUIT

#30 STORM WINDOW MEMBER*

CORNER LOCK*
(4 REQ'D)

.437

.768

TYPICAL CROSS·SECTION

* REYNOLDS METAL CO'S "DO-IT-YOURSELF ALUMINUM

77

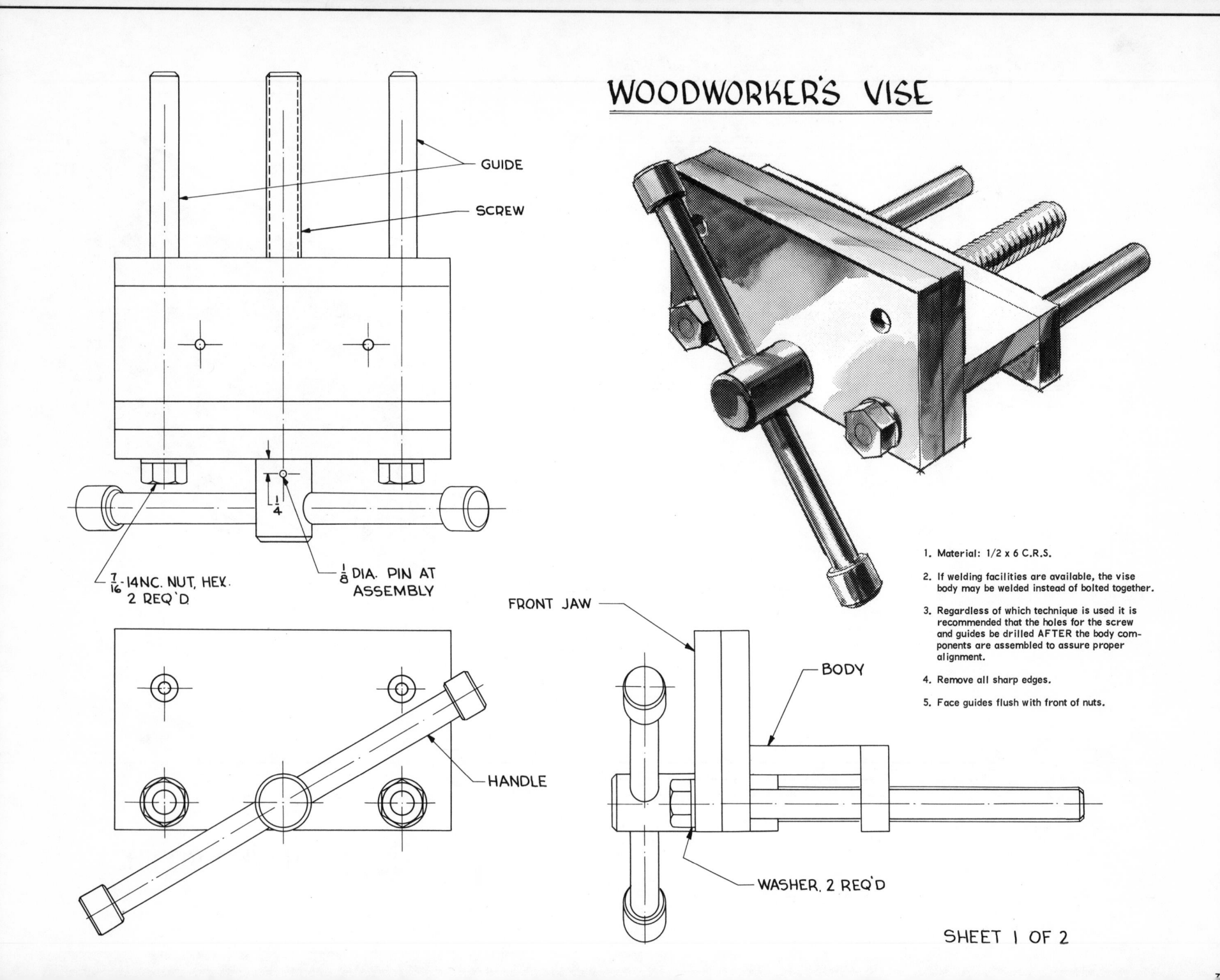

WOODWORKER'S VISE

GUIDE

SCREW

$\frac{7}{16}$-14NC. NUT, HEX.
2 REQ'D

$\frac{1}{8}$ DIA. PIN AT
ASSEMBLY

$\frac{1}{4}$

HANDLE

FRONT JAW

BODY

WASHER. 2 REQ'D

1. Material: 1/2 x 6 C.R.S.

2. If welding facilities are available, the vise body may be welded instead of bolted together.

3. Regardless of which technique is used it is recommended that the holes for the screw and guides be drilled AFTER the body components are assembled to assure proper alignment.

4. Remove all sharp edges.

5. Face guides flush with front of nuts.

SHEET 1 OF 2

70

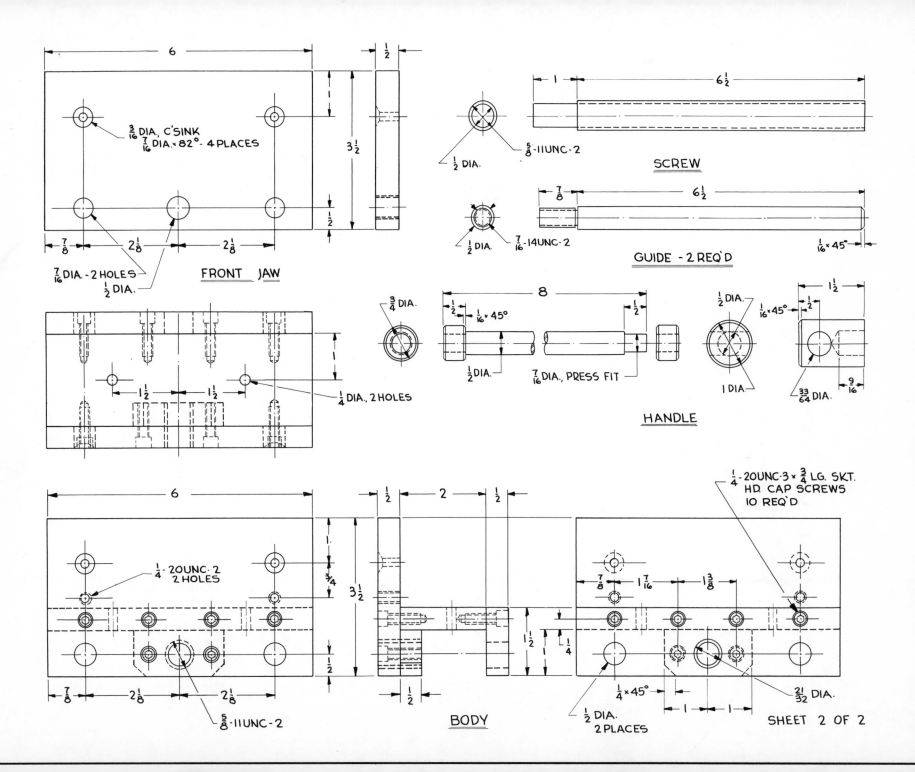

$\frac{3}{16}$ DIA., C'SINK
$\frac{7}{16}$ DIA. × 82° - 4 PLACES

6

$\frac{1}{2}$

$3\frac{1}{2}$

$\frac{1}{2}$

$\frac{7}{8}$ $2\frac{1}{8}$ $2\frac{1}{8}$

$\frac{7}{16}$ DIA. - 2 HOLES
$\frac{1}{2}$ DIA.

FRONT JAW

$\frac{1}{2}$ DIA.

$\frac{5}{8}$-11UNC-2

SCREW

1   $6\frac{1}{2}$

$\frac{7}{8}$ $6\frac{1}{2}$

$\frac{1}{2}$ DIA. $\frac{7}{16}$-14UNC-2

$\frac{1}{16}$ × 45°

GUIDE - 2 REQ'D

$1\frac{1}{2}$ $1\frac{1}{2}$

$\frac{1}{4}$ DIA., 2 HOLES

$\frac{3}{4}$ DIA.

8

$\frac{1}{2}$ $\frac{1}{16}$ × 45° $\frac{1}{2}$

$\frac{1}{2}$ DIA. $\frac{7}{16}$ DIA., PRESS FIT

$\frac{1}{2}$ DIA. $\frac{1}{16}$ × 45° $\frac{1}{2}$

$1\frac{1}{2}$

1 DIA. $\frac{33}{64}$ DIA. $\frac{9}{16}$

HANDLE

6

$\frac{1}{2}$ 2 $\frac{1}{2}$

$\frac{1}{4}$ - 20UNC- 2
2 HOLES

1.

$\frac{3}{4}$

$3\frac{1}{2}$

$\frac{1}{2}$

$\frac{7}{8}$ $2\frac{1}{8}$ $2\frac{1}{8}$

$\frac{5}{8}$-11UNC-2

$\frac{1}{2}$

BODY

$\frac{1}{4}$ - 20UNC-3 × $\frac{3}{4}$ LG. SKT.
HD. CAP SCREWS
10 REQ'D

$\frac{7}{8}$ $1\frac{7}{16}$ $1\frac{3}{8}$

$1\frac{1}{2}$ $\frac{1}{4}$

$\frac{1}{4}$ × 45°   1   1

$\frac{1}{2}$ DIA.
2 PLACES

$\frac{21}{32}$ DIA.

SHEET 2 OF 2

HAT & COAT HANGER

1. Material: 1/8 brass or aluminum.

2. Finish: High polish.

3. Round all edges.

4. Rack to mount hangers is made from 3/4 walnut six inches wide and as long as necessary to mount the desired number of hangers on six inch centers.

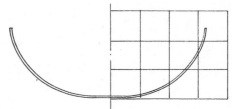

SECTION B-B

½ SQUARES

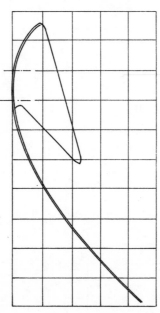

SECTION A-A

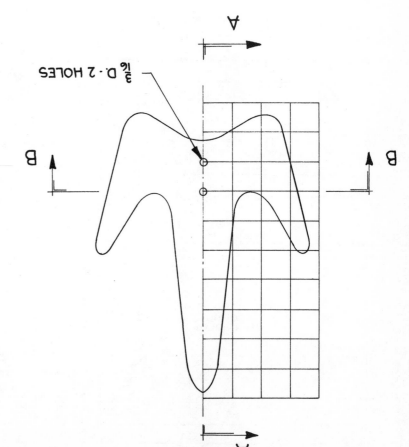

$\frac{3}{16}$ D - 2 HOLES

A

B

B

A

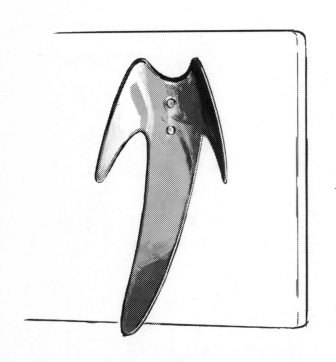

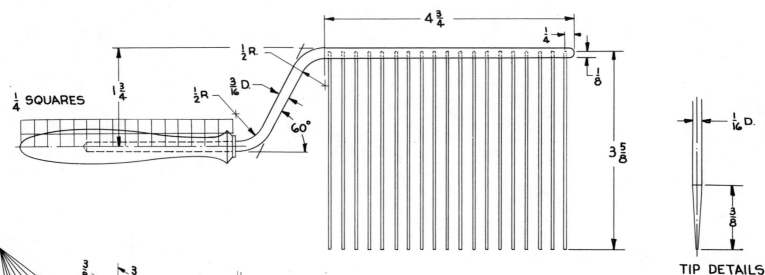

¼ SQUARES

4 ¾

½ R.

1 ¾

¾₁₆ D.

½ R.

60°

¼

⅛

3 ⅝

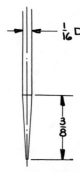

TIP DETAILS

1/16 D.

3/8

¼

3/8 3/4

3/4

2

¼ D. 1/16 D. - 7 HOLES

GUIDE PIN

DRILL JIG

CAKE KNIFE

1. Material: Metal parts – Stainless steel welding rod.
   Handle – Walnut, ebony or plastic.

2. Finish: Polished.

3. Silver solder tines into drilled holes.

4. Epoxy cement handle to frame.

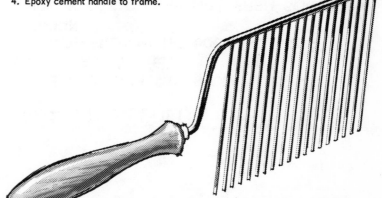

USING THE DRILL JIG:

1. Measure in 1/4 inch from the frame end and drill a 1/16 dia.
   hole by 3/32 deep.

2. Insert rod into jig until the guide pin slips into the previously
   drilled hole.

3. Insert drill in chuck and adjust drill press to permit the drill to
   cut to the required depth.

4. Drill the six (6) 1/16 dia. holes permitted by the jig.

5. Repeat operation until the required number of holes are drilled.

PROBLEM: DESIGN A SET OF BOOK ENDS

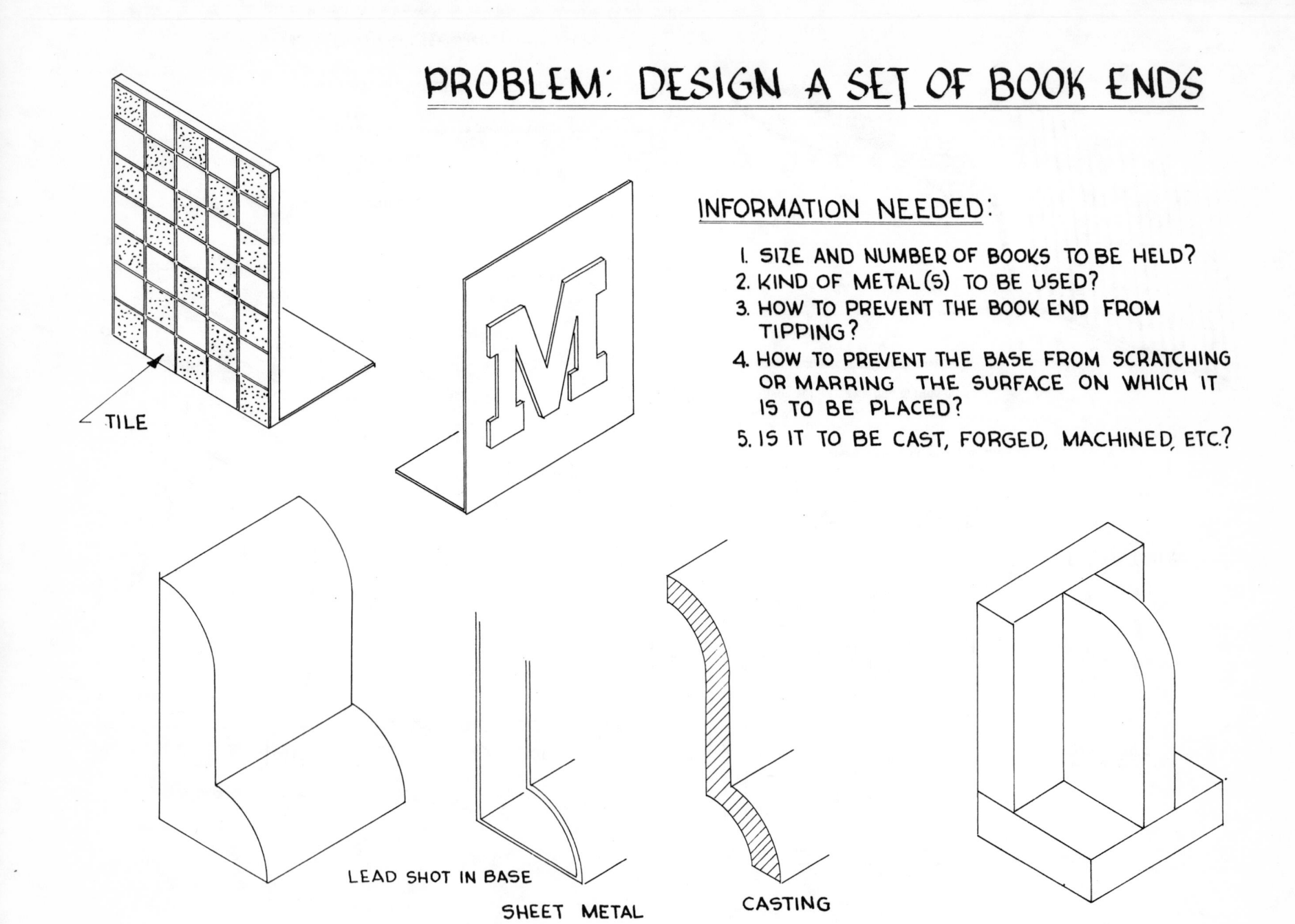

INFORMATION NEEDED:

1. SIZE AND NUMBER OF BOOKS TO BE HELD?
2. KIND OF METAL(S) TO BE USED?
3. HOW TO PREVENT THE BOOK END FROM TIPPING?
4. HOW TO PREVENT THE BASE FROM SCRATCHING OR MARRING THE SURFACE ON WHICH IT IS TO BE PLACED?
5. IS IT TO BE CAST, FORGED, MACHINED, ETC.?

TILE

LEAD SHOT IN BASE

SHEET METAL

CASTING

WOOD HOLDER

1. Material: Supports - hot rolled steel.
   Body - brass or aluminum (16 or 18 ga.).

2. Finish: Supports - paint flat black.
   Body - polished or satin finish.

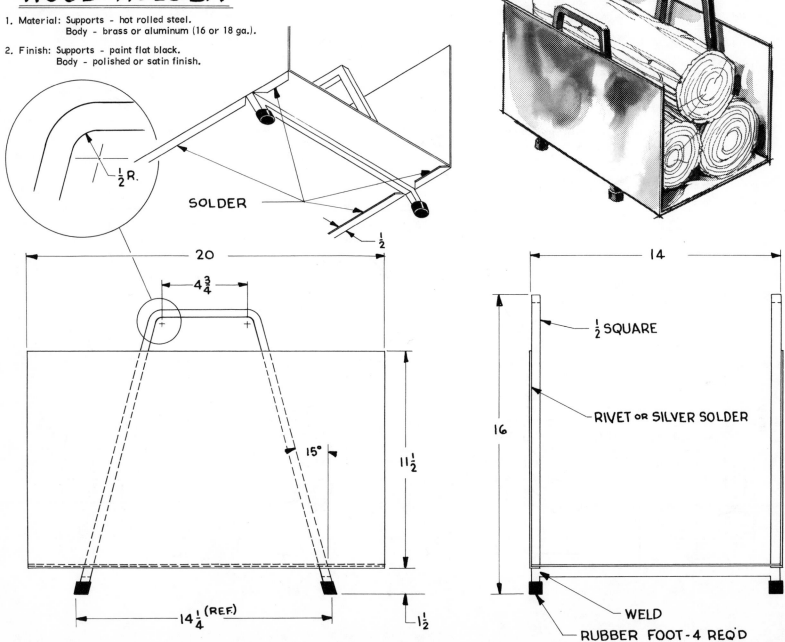

$\frac{1}{2}$ R.

SOLDER

$\frac{1}{2}$

20

$4\frac{3}{4}$

15°

$11\frac{1}{2}$

$14\frac{1}{4}$ (REF.)

$1\frac{1}{2}$

14

$\frac{1}{2}$ SQUARE

16

RIVET OR SILVER SOLDER

WELD

RUBBER FOOT - 4 REQ'D

DOOR NUMBERS

1. Material: 1/8 inch copper if the mounting plate is to be brass. However, any two contrasting metals are suitable.

2. Finish: Polished. If copper and brass are used, spray the CLEANED polished surface with clear spray plastic.

3. Mount the numbers to the plate by soldering (hard or soft). Aluminum numbers can be mounted with #2-56NC x 1/4 long machine screws that are obtainable at most hobby shops.

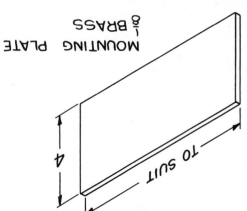

MOUNTING PLATE $\frac{1}{8}$ BRASS

4

TO SUIT

$\frac{1}{2}$ INCH SQUARES

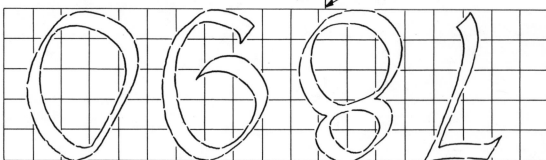

7 8 9 0

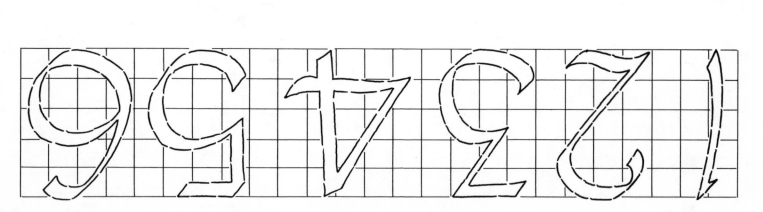

1 2 3 4 5 6

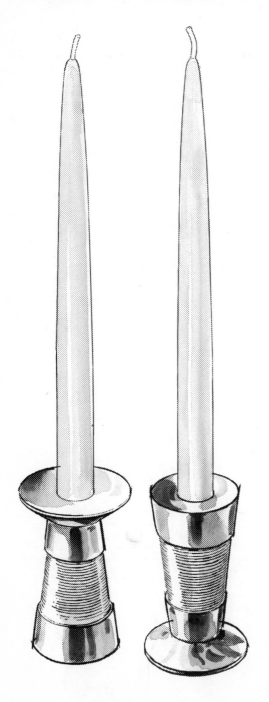

REVERSIBLE CANDLE HOLDER

NOTE:

1. Material: Aluminum, brass or pewter.

2. Finish: Polish.

3. Remove all sharp edges and burrs.

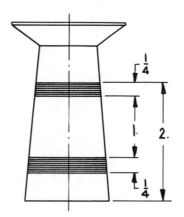

ALTERNATE DESIGN

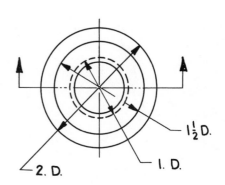

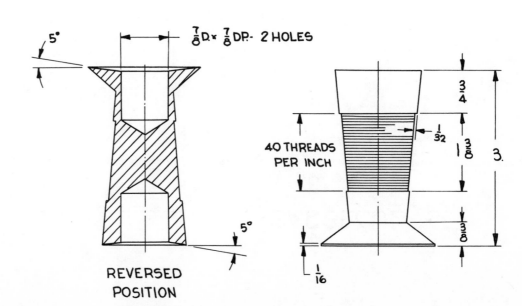

REVERSED POSITION

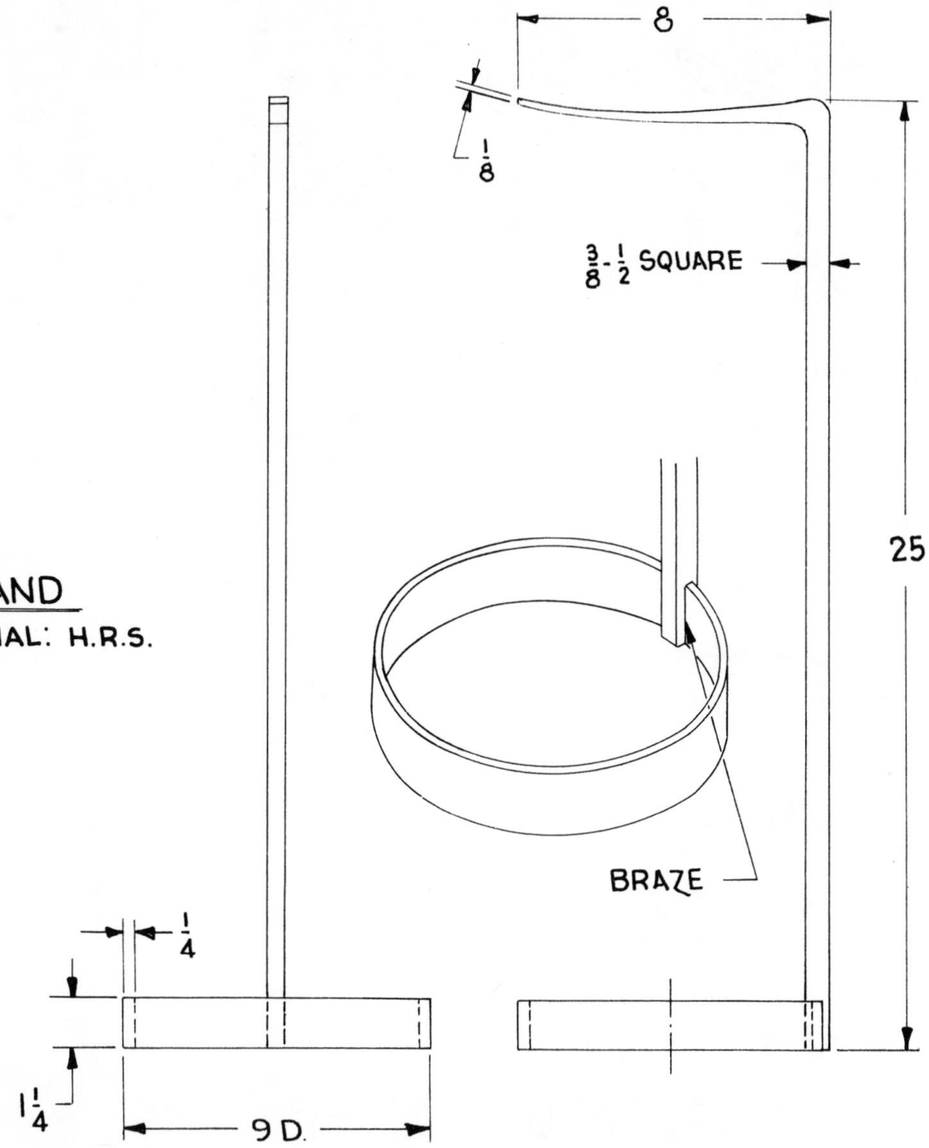

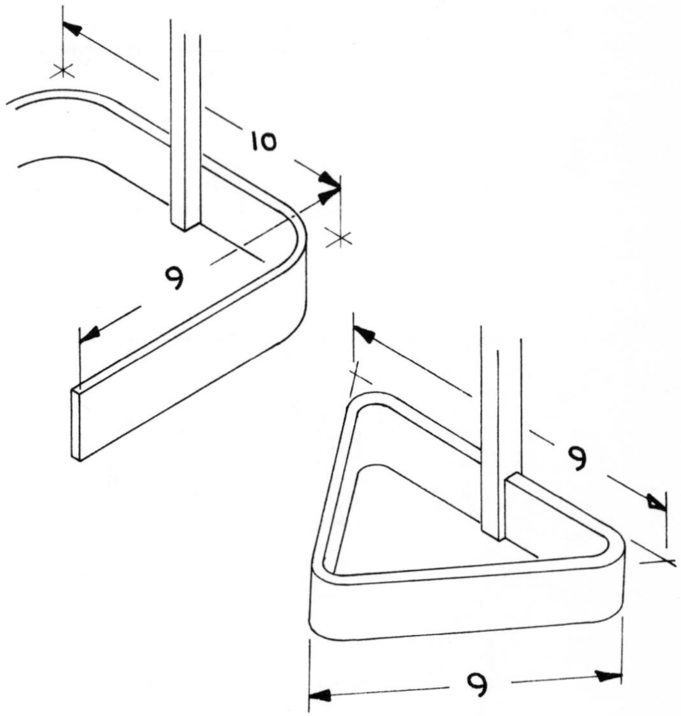

ALTERNATE BASE DESIGNS

6

6

6

4

10

BARBECUE SET

1. Material: As noted.

2. Finish: Stand – Burnt linseed oil or paint flat black. Others: Natural.

3. Remove all sharp edges.

25

BRAZE

$3\frac{3}{8} - \frac{1}{2}$ SQUARE

8

$\frac{1}{8}$

STAND

MATERIAL: H.R.S.

9 D

$1\frac{1}{4}$

$\frac{1}{4}$

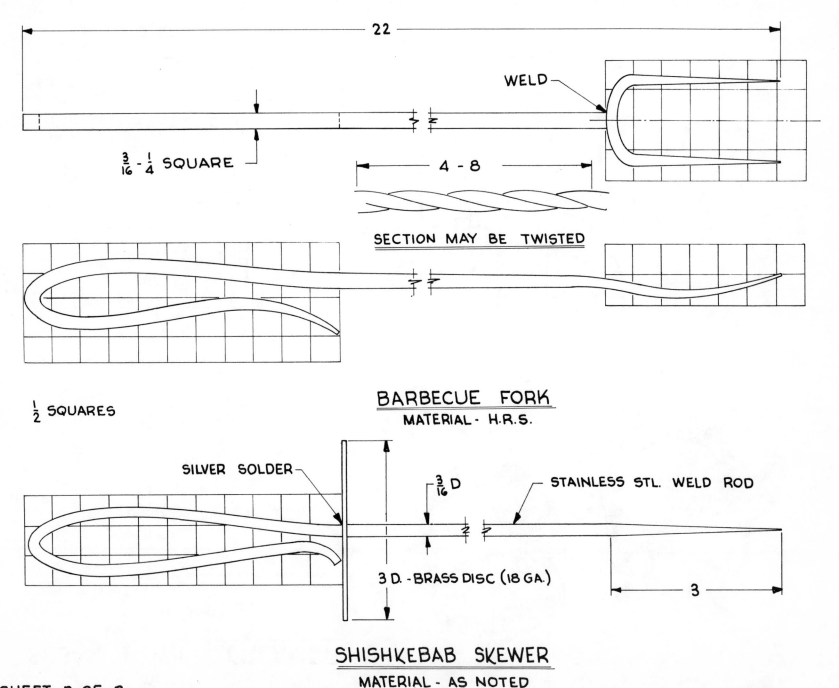

22

WELD

$\frac{3}{16} - \frac{1}{4}$ SQUARE

4 - 8

SECTION MAY BE TWISTED

$\frac{1}{2}$ SQUARES

BARBECUE FORK
MATERIAL - H.R.S.

SILVER SOLDER

$\frac{3}{16}$ D

STAINLESS STL. WELD ROD

3 D. - BRASS DISC (18 GA.)

3

SHISHKEBAB SKEWER
MATERIAL - AS NOTED

SHEET 2 OF 2

SUGAR BOWL & CREAMER

1. Material: 18 ga. pewter or brass.

2. Use 60-40 solder when working pewter (professional-like results can be obtained by fusing the joints with snippets of pewter instead of solder).

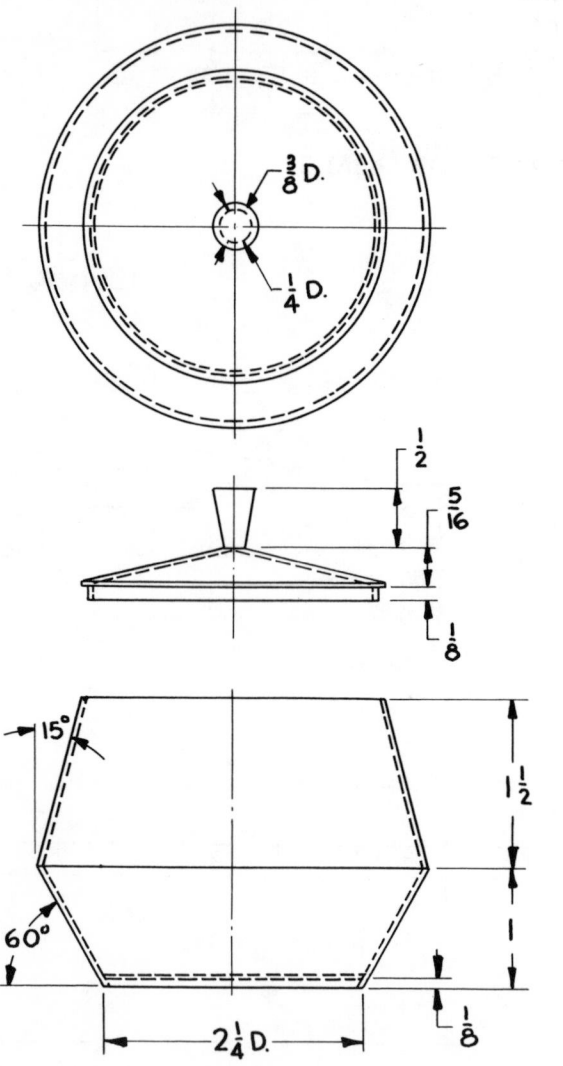

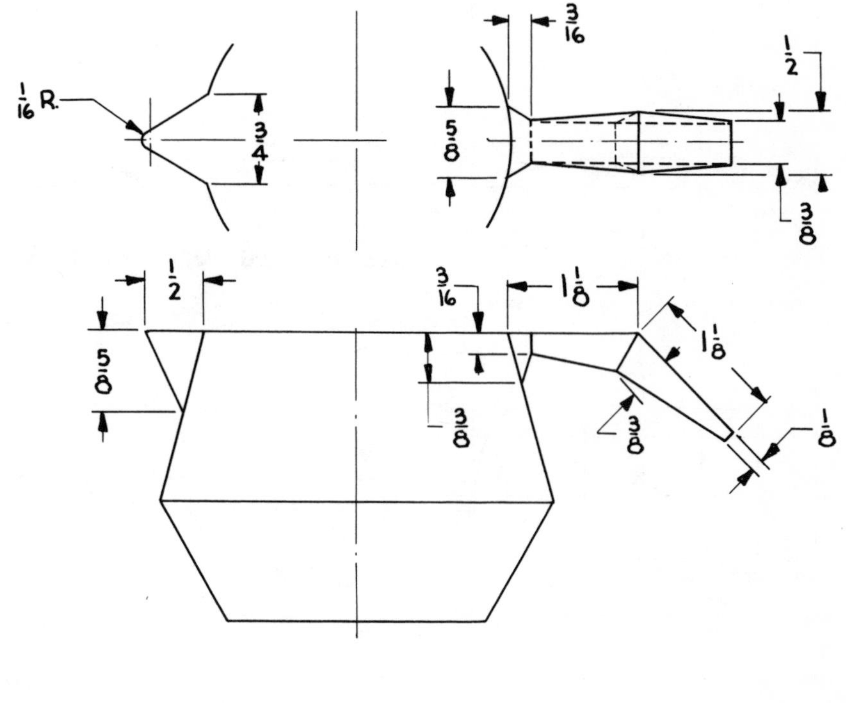

$\frac{3}{8}$ D.

$\frac{1}{4}$ D.

$\frac{1}{2}$

$\frac{5}{16}$

$\frac{1}{8}$

15°

60°

$1\frac{1}{2}$

$2\frac{1}{4}$ D.

$\frac{1}{8}$

$\frac{1}{16}$ R.

$\frac{3}{4}$

$\frac{3}{16}$

$\frac{1}{2}$

$\frac{5}{8}$

$\frac{3}{8}$

$\frac{1}{2}$

$\frac{5}{8}$

$\frac{3}{16}$

$1\frac{1}{8}$

$1\frac{1}{8}$

$\frac{3}{8}$

$\frac{3}{8}$

$\frac{1}{8}$

PENCIL HOLDER

A project of this nature permits the student to attempt a bit of elementary design work. A few ideas already tried are:

A. Wrapping the undercut with twine or cord or copper or brass wire. If wire is used it is suggested that a hole the diameter of the wire be drilled at the start and finish of the winding. The wrapping can be held in place with an epoxy adhesive.

B. A square nosed tool 1/8 wide was used to cut this pattern. The cut is 1/16 deep.

C. This pattern was cut using a tool with a 1/16 radius ground on its nose. The cut is 1/16 deep.

D. Interesting and attractive designs can be made by cementing leather, cloth and the like in the undercut.

The basic project is made from aluminum - cast or bar stock. Aluminum pipe can be used if a shoulder is cut in the base to permit a bottom to be shrink fitted into place.

Follow instructions carefully when using epoxy adhesives in order to secure maximum holding strength.

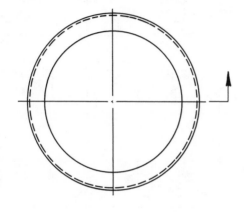

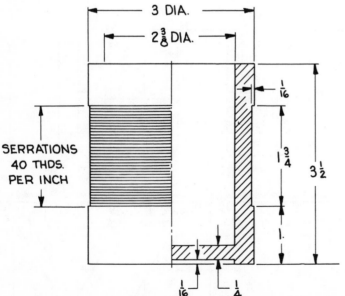

3 DIA.

2 3/8 DIA.

SERRATIONS
40 THDS.
PER INCH

1/16

1 3/4

3 1/2

1.

1/16   1/4

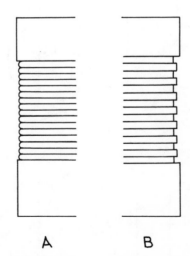

A   B   C   D

ALTERNATE PATTERN IDEAS

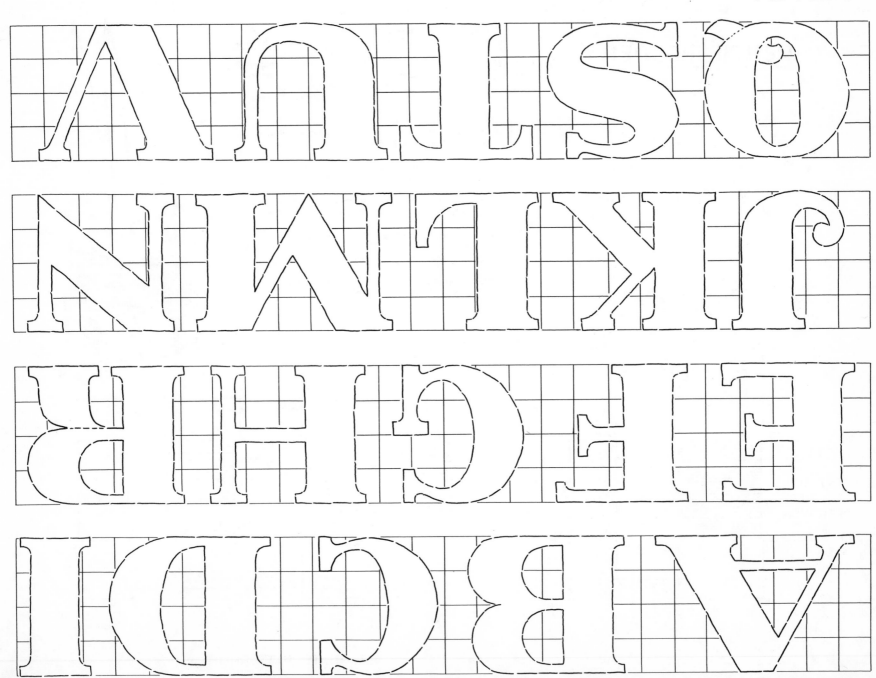

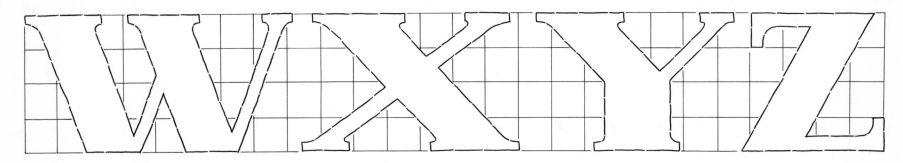

PAPER WEIGHT - 1 INCH SQUARES
BOOK END - 1½ INCH SQUARES

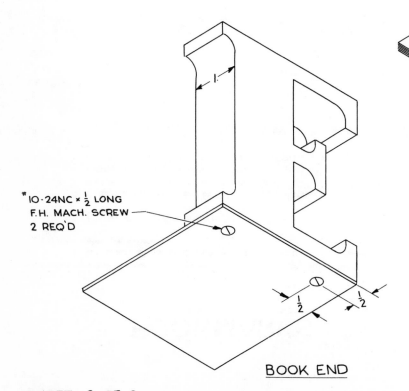

\# 10-24NC × ½ LONG
F.H. MACH. SCREW
2 REQ'D

½   ½

BOOK END

PAPER WEIGHT

MONOGRAM

BOOK ENDS

1. Material: Cast aluminum.

2. Finish: As cast, polished or flat black paint.

3. Bottom plate: .040 half-hard aluminum.

PAPER WEIGHT

1. Material: Brass or aluminum.

2. Finish: Polished.

3. Cement felt to bottom of monogram.

SHEET 2 OF 2

91

SILVER SOLDER

¼ SQUARES

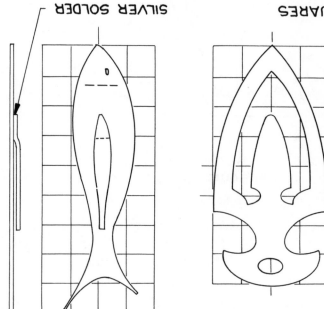

3. Enameling may be used to give a more colorful appearance. Pennsylvania German motifs (hex signs) offer many possibilities of being in- corporated into an original design bookmark.

2. Finish: Polished or satin finish.

1. Material: 20 ga. brass, copper, aluminum or sterling silver.

BOOKMARKS

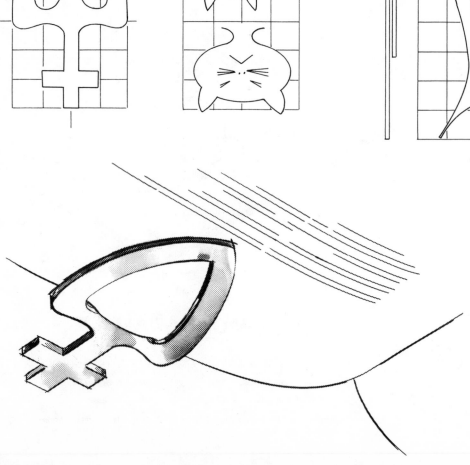

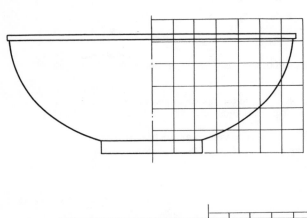

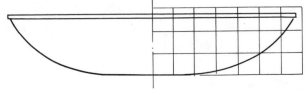

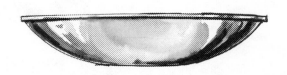

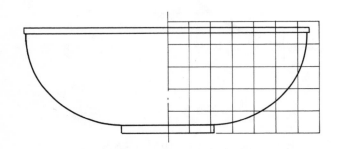

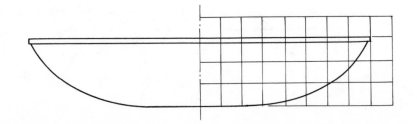

CONTEMPORARY BOWLS

1. Material: Sterling, pewter, aluminum, copper or brass.

2. Finish: Polished exterior, matt interior.

3. Size: 10 inches to 15 inches in diameter.

CANDLE SNUFFER

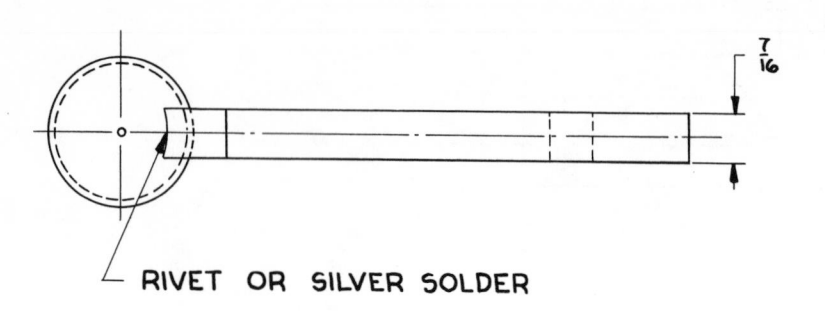

$\frac{7}{16}$

RIVET OR SILVER SOLDER

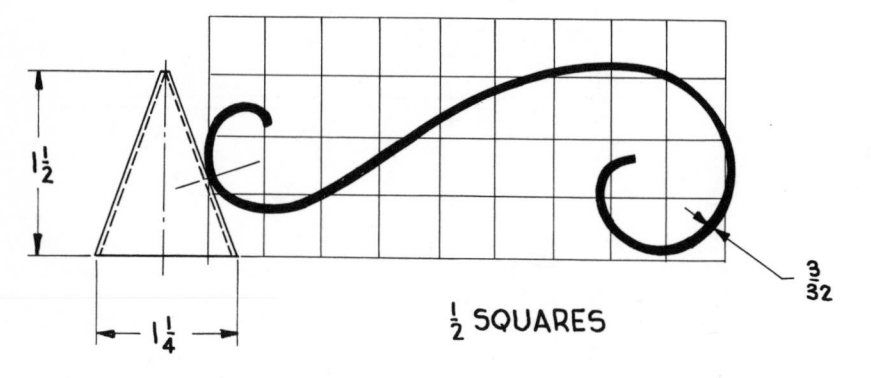

$1\frac{1}{2}$

$1\frac{1}{4}$

$\frac{1}{2}$ SQUARES

$\frac{3}{32}$

1. Material: Snuffer – 20 ga. brass, copper or black annealed steel
   sheet. Handle – 7/16 wide by 1/16 or 3/32 thick.

2. Finish: Brass and copper should be polished and sprayed with clear
   lacquer to prevent oxidation. Paint the black annealed steel
   sheet flat black.

3. Problem: Develop a manufacturing technique to produce the conical
   snuffer.

SERRATED PEN HOLDER BASE

1. Material: Aluminum, brass, stainless steel or C.F.S.

2. Finish: Satin finish or polish as desired.

3. Remove all burrs and sharp edges.

4. Cover bottom with felt.

5. Pen and pen holder available from most school shop supply sources.

$\frac{9}{64}$ D., C'SINK $\frac{3}{8}$ D × 82°

45°   45°

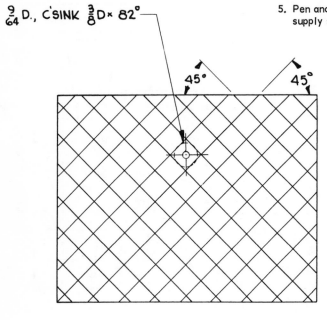

$4\frac{1}{2}$

$2\frac{1}{4}$

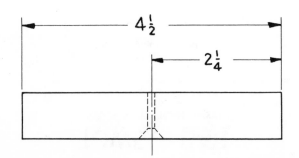

3

1

$\frac{3}{4}$

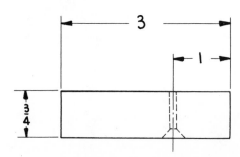

90° $\frac{3}{8}$ $\frac{1}{32}$

ENLARGED SECTION THROUGH SERRATIONS

TOWEL BAR
(EARLY AMERICAN MOTIF)

1. Material: Aluminum, brass or annealed steel sheet.

2. Finish: Aluminum and brass - polished.
   Steel - paint flat black.

3. Remove all sharp edges.

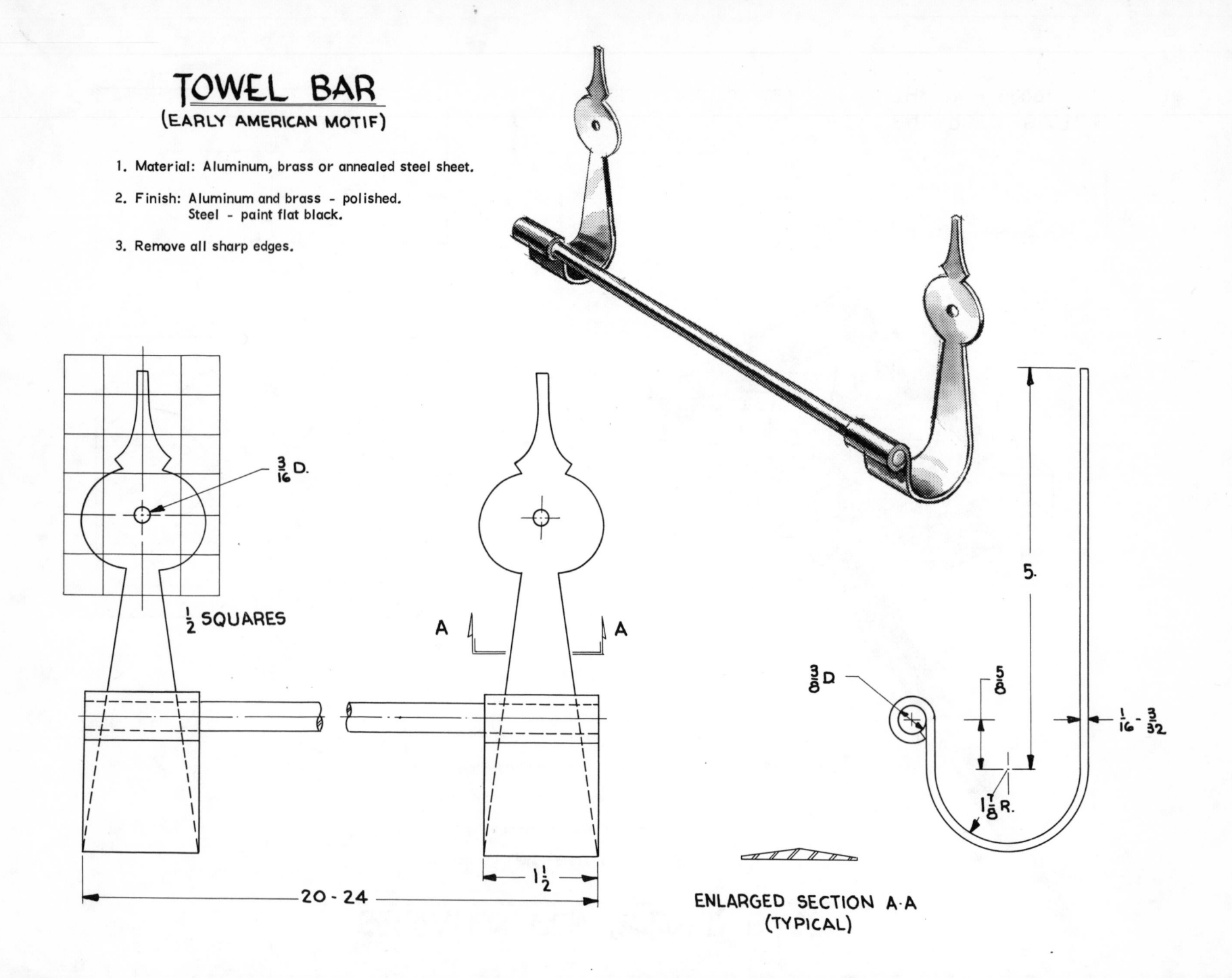

$\frac{3}{16}$ D.

$\frac{1}{2}$ SQUARES

20 - 24

$1\frac{1}{2}$

A   A

5.

$\frac{3}{8}$ D.

$\frac{5}{8}$

$\frac{1}{16} - \frac{3}{32}$

$1\frac{7}{8}$ R.

ENLARGED SECTION A·A
(TYPICAL)

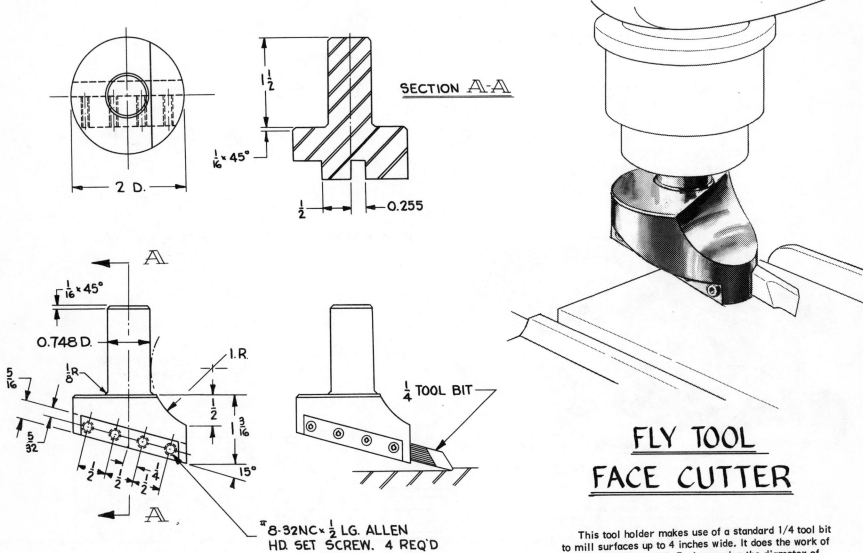

SECTION A-A

$\frac{1}{6} \times 45°$

2 D.

$1\frac{1}{2}$

$\frac{1}{2}$ — 0.255

A

$\frac{1}{16} \times 45°$

0.748 D.

$\frac{5}{16}$

$\frac{1}{8}$ R

$\frac{5}{32}$

1. R.

$\frac{1}{2}$

$\frac{3}{16}$

15°

$\frac{1}{2}$ $\frac{1}{2}$ $\frac{1}{4}$ $\frac{1}{2}$

A

#8·32NC × $\frac{1}{2}$ LG. ALLEN
HD. SET SCREW. 4 REQ'D

$\frac{1}{4}$ TOOL BIT

FLY TOOL
FACE CUTTER

This tool holder makes use of a standard 1/4 tool bit
to mill surfaces up to 4 inches wide. It does the work of
an expensive face mill. By increasing the diameter of
the body and the width of the slot, wider surfaces can be
milled. The tool is counterbalanced to cut smoother.

NOTE:

1. Material: C.R.S.

2. Break all sharp edges. Remove all burrs.

UNLESS OTHERWISE SPECIFIED:
DIMENSIONAL TOLERANCES-
    FRACTIONAL ± $\frac{1}{64}$
    DECIMAL ± .003
    ANGULAR ± 2°

DAHLGREN "SODA BOTTLE" CANNON

This muzzle loading smooth bore cannon was designed in 1850 by John Dahlgren for the Royal Navy. It was made of cast iron and its shape, which looked like the sodawater bottle of that time, was determined by the careful study of the pressure that developed inside the gun when it was fired. Dahlgren made it thick where great pressures developed and thin where the thickness was not of great importance.

TOUCH HOLE

#2 × ½ RH. BRASS WD. SCREW. 4 REQ'D.

$\frac{1}{16}$ DIA. × $\frac{1}{2}$ PIN 2 REQ'D

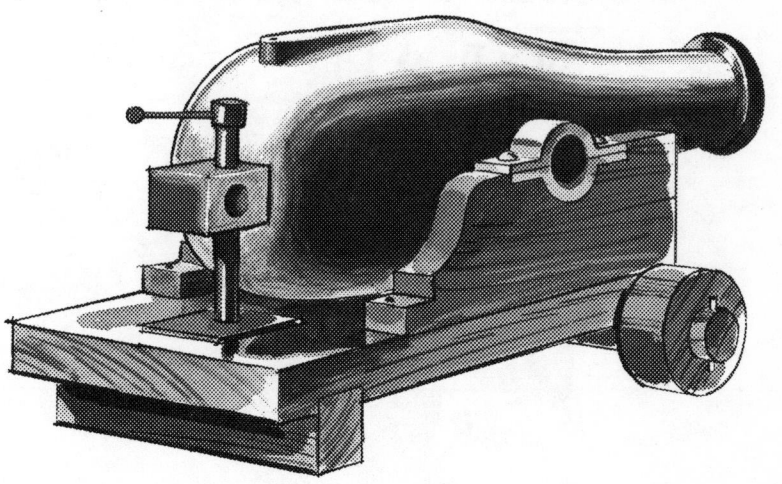

ELEVATING SCREW

TRUNNION BEARING

CARRIAGE

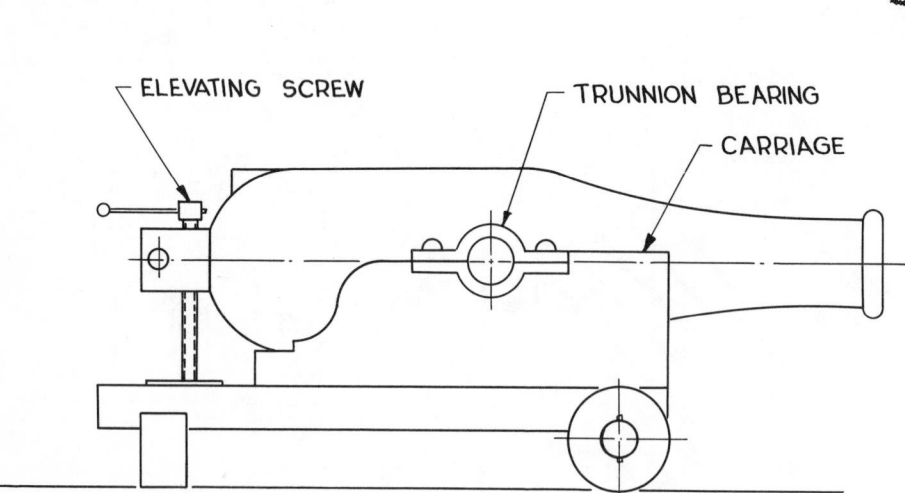

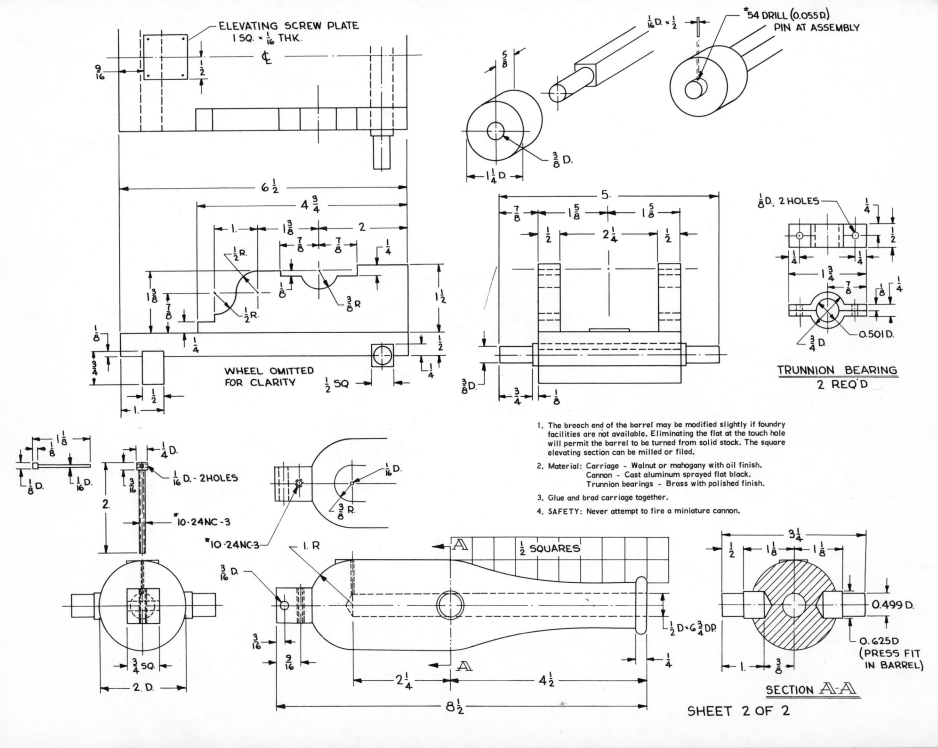

ELEVATING SCREW PLATE
1 SQ. × 1/16 THK.

#54 DRILL (0.055 D)
PIN AT ASSEMBLY

WHEEL OMITTED
FOR CLARITY

1/2 SQ

TRUNNION BEARING
2 REQ'D

0.501 D.

1/8 D., 2 HOLES

1. The breech end of the barrel may be modified slightly if foundry facilities are not available. Eliminating the flat at the touch hole will permit the barrel to be turned from solid stock. The square elevating section can be milled or filed.

2. Material: Carriage - Walnut or mahogany with oil finish.
   Cannon - Cast aluminum sprayed flat black.
   Trunnion bearings - Brass with polished finish.

3. Glue and brad carriage together.

4. SAFETY: Never attempt to fire a miniature cannon.

#10-24NC-3

1/16 D. - 2 HOLES

3/4 SQ.

2. D.

1. R

3/16 D.

1/2 D × 6 3/4 DP.

1/2 SQUARES

0.499 D.

0.625 D.
(PRESS FIT
IN BARREL)

SECTION A-A

SHEET 2 OF 2

1. Material: Sterling or nickel silver.

2. Finish: Polished or satin finish.

3. Attach ornamentation with silver solder.

4. Remove all burrs and sharp edges.

ALTERNATE DESIGNS

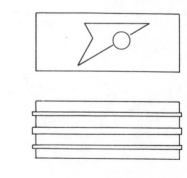

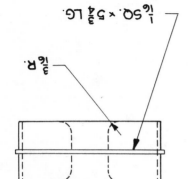

1½ SQ. × 5⅜ LG.

³⁄₃₂ R

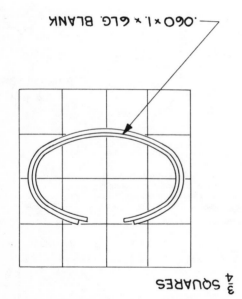

.060 × 1 × 6 LG. BLANK

¾ SQUARES

BRACELET

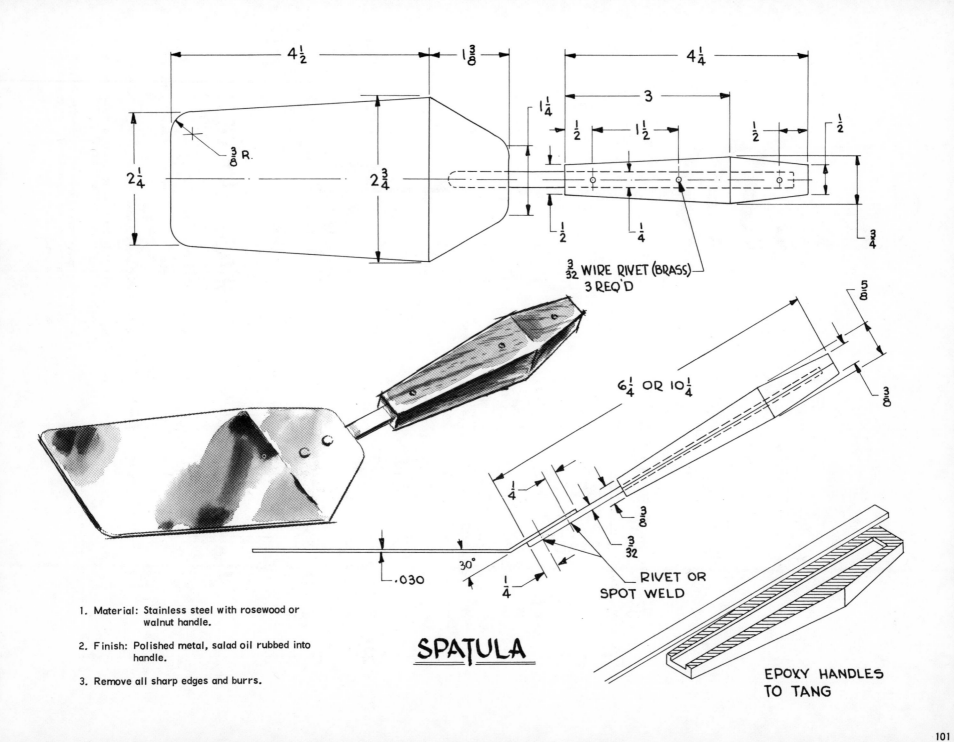

4½ · 1⅜ · 4¼

3

1¼ · ½ · 1½ · ½ · ½

⅜ R.

2¼ · 2¾

½ · ¼ · ¾

³⁄₃₂ WIRE RIVET (BRASS)
3 REQ'D

5⁄8 · 3⁄8

6¼ OR 10¼

¼ · 3⁄8 · ³⁄₃₂

.030 · 30° · ¼

RIVET OR
SPOT WELD

1. Material: Stainless steel with rosewood or
   walnut handle.

2. Finish: Polished metal, salad oil rubbed into
   handle.

3. Remove all sharp edges and burrs.

SPATULA

EPOXY HANDLES
TO TANG

GLASS HOLDER

1. Material: 3/16 dia. rod.

2. Finish: Paint bright color or cover rod with patterned plastic tubing.

3. Remove all sharp edges.

4. Advanced metals classes can develop a manufacturing technique to produce a uniform spiral.

5. The glass holder may be spun and attached to the rod by threading the end and using two hex nuts or may be brazed to the rod.

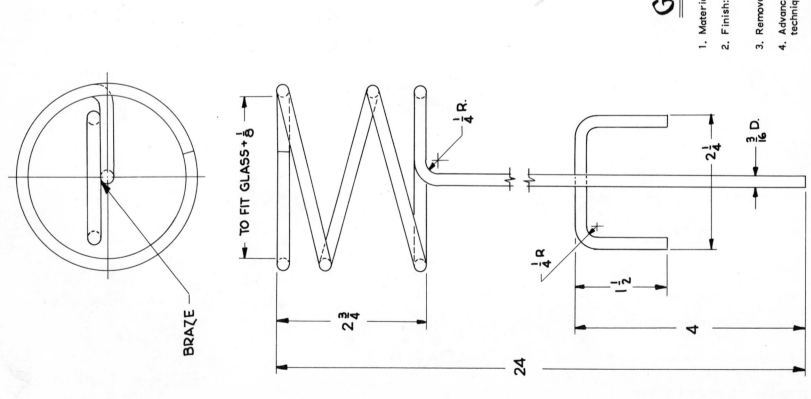

BRAZE

TO FIT GLASS + $\frac{1}{8}$

$2\frac{3}{4}$

$\frac{1}{4}$ R.

$\frac{1}{4}$ R

$2\frac{1}{4}$

$\frac{3}{16}$ D.

$1\frac{1}{2}$

4

24

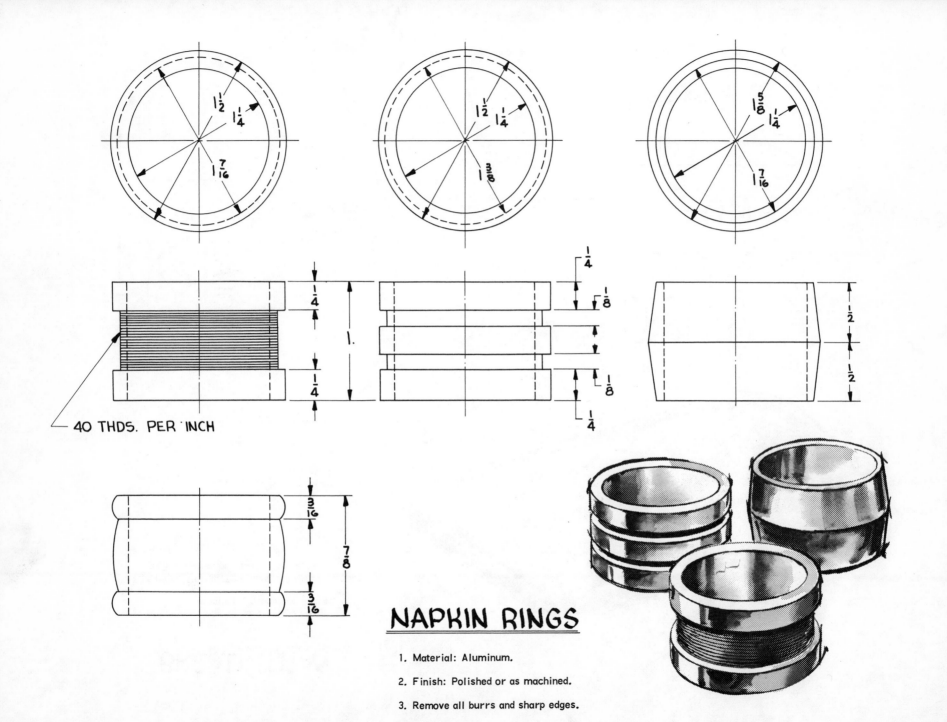

40 THDS. PER INCH

$1\frac{1}{2}$ $1\frac{1}{4}$

$1\frac{7}{16}$

$1\frac{1}{2}$ $1\frac{1}{4}$

$1\frac{3}{8}$

$1\frac{5}{8}$ $1\frac{1}{4}$

$1\frac{7}{16}$

$\frac{1}{4}$ 1. $\frac{1}{4}$

$\frac{1}{4}$ $\frac{1}{8}$ $\frac{1}{8}$ $\frac{1}{4}$

$\frac{1}{2}$ $\frac{1}{2}$

$\frac{3}{16}$ $\frac{7}{8}$ $\frac{3}{16}$

NAPKIN RINGS

1. Material: Aluminum.

2. Finish: Polished or as machined.

3. Remove all burrs and sharp edges.

103

SECTION A-A

⅜ SQUARES

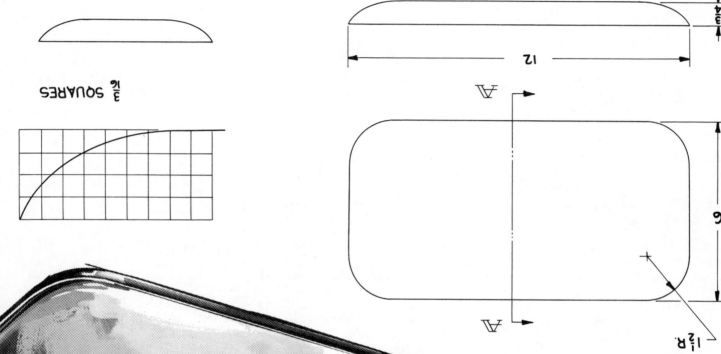

12

¾

6

1½R

A   A

BREAD TRAY

1. Material: 18 or 20 ga. sterling silver, pewter, aluminum, copper or brass.

2. Finish: Planish (not peen) the entire surface until smooth then polish.

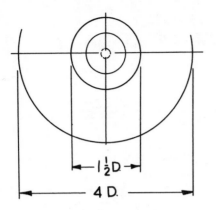

CONTEMPORARY CANDLE HOLDER

1. Material: Aluminum, brass or C.R.S.
   Finish: Polished or painted flat black.

2. Remove all burrs and sharp edges.

3. Cover bottom of base with felt or cork.

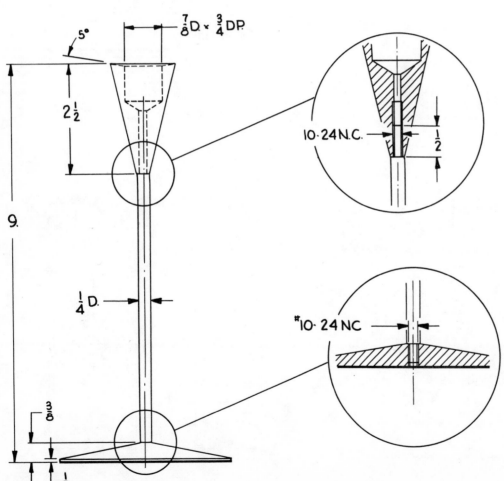

$1\frac{1}{2}$ D.

4 D.

5°

$\frac{7}{8}$ D. × $\frac{3}{4}$ DP.

$2\frac{1}{2}$

9.

$\frac{1}{4}$ D.

$\frac{3}{8}$

$\frac{1}{16}$

10·24 N.C.

$\frac{1}{2}$

#10·24 NC

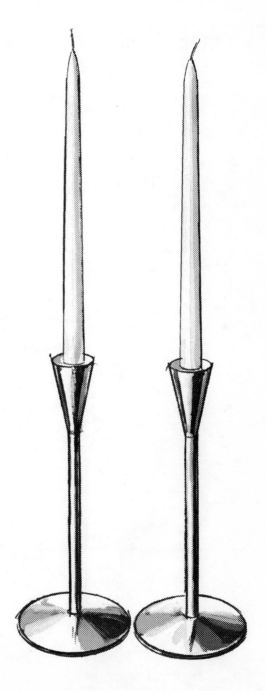

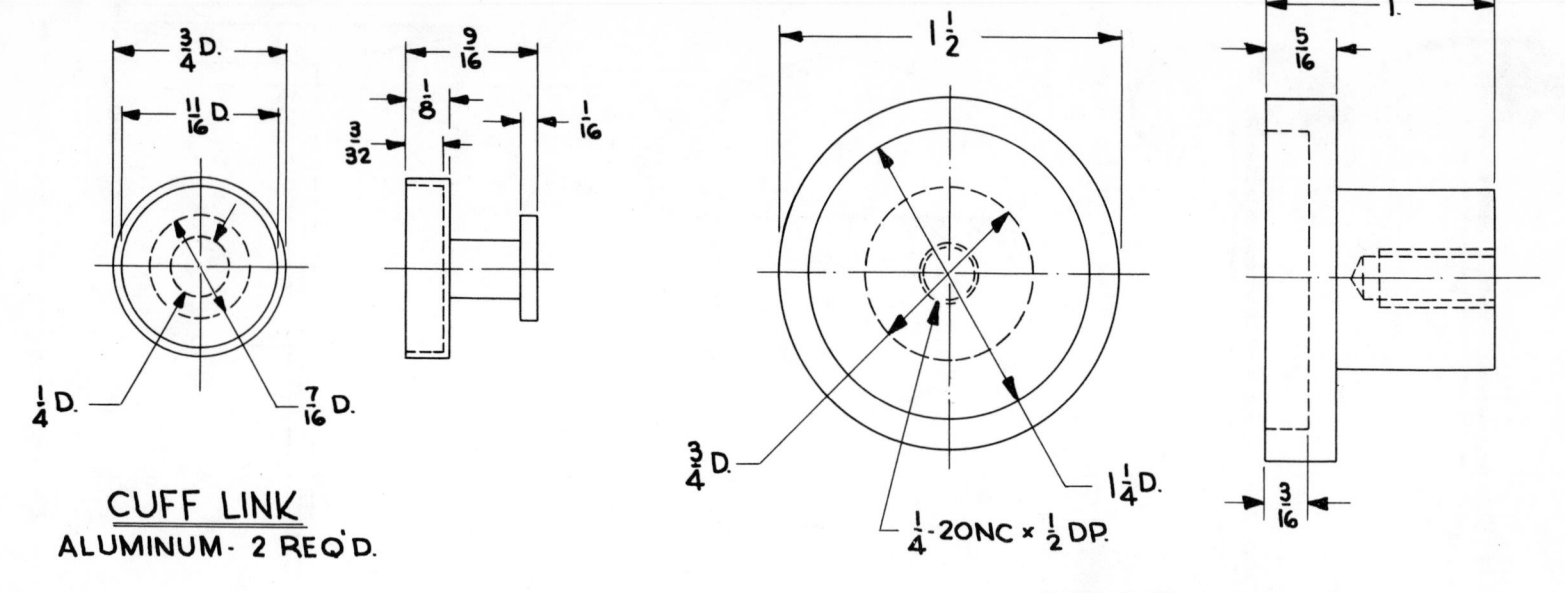

CUFF LINK
ALUMINUM - 2 REQ'D.

DRAWER PULLS
ALUMINUM -

$\frac{1}{4}$-20NC × $\frac{1}{2}$ DP.

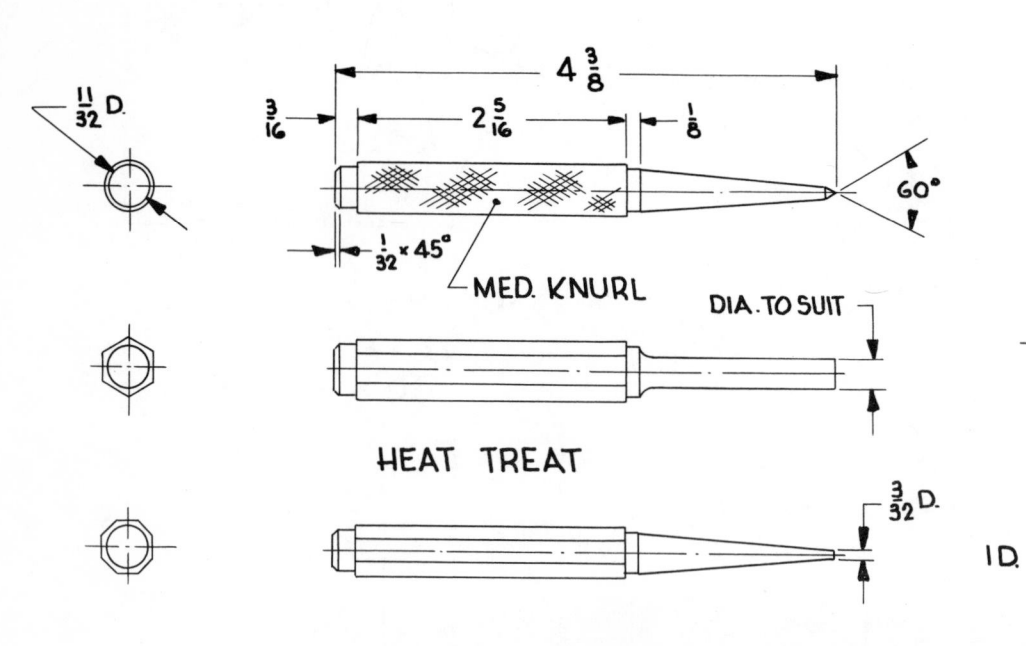

MED. KNURL

HEAT TREAT

DIA. TO SUIT

PUNCHES, CENTER, PIN, DRIFT
$\frac{3}{8}$ TOOL STEEL

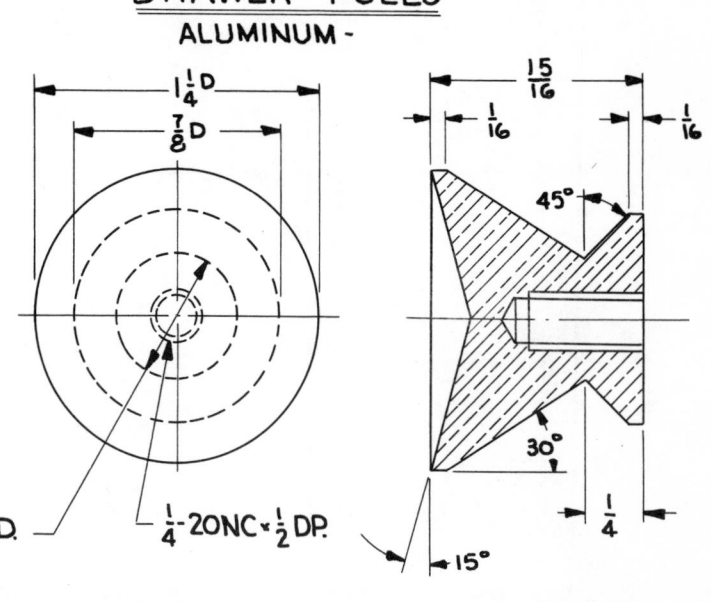

$\frac{1}{4}$-20NC × $\frac{1}{2}$ DP.

"QUICKIE" LATHE PROJECTS

SPUR GEAR PEN HOLDER BASE

1. Material: Aluminum, brass, stainless steel or C.F.S.

2. Finish: Satin finish or polished as desired.

3. Remove all sharp edges and burrs.

4. Cover bottom with felt.

5. Pen and pen holder available from most school shop supply sources.

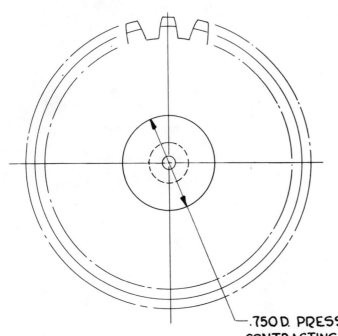

.750 D. PRESS FIT.
CONTRASTING MATERIAL

$\frac{9}{64}$ D. - C'SINK $\frac{1}{4}$ D. ×82°

30°

$\frac{1}{2}$

GEAR DATA	
OUTSIDE DIA.	2.500
NO. OF TEETH	28
PRESSURE ANGLE	14° 30'
PITCH DIA.	2.333
WHOLE DEPTH	.180
DIAMETRAL PITCH	12

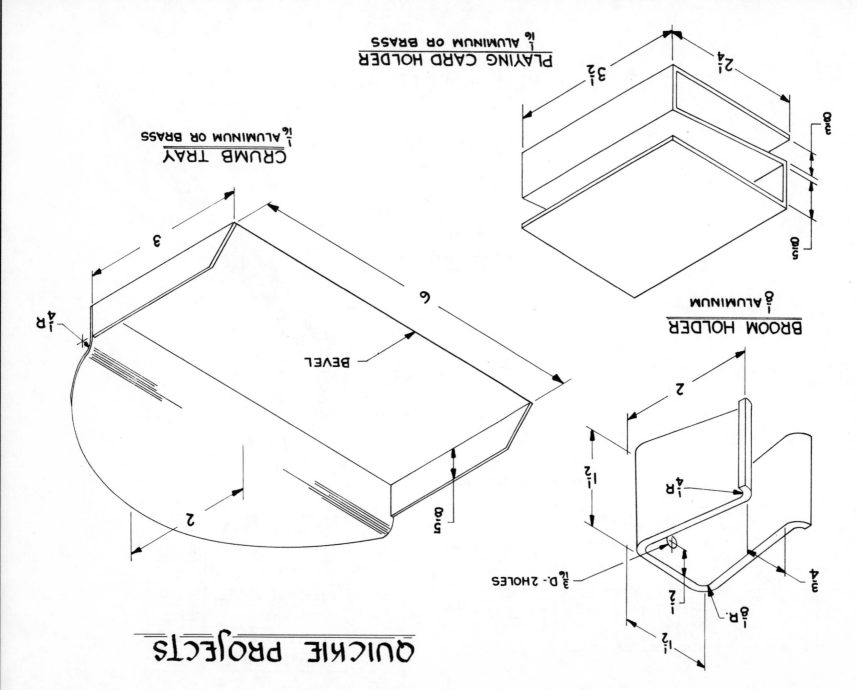

PLAYING CARD HOLDER
$\frac{1}{16}$ ALUMINUM OR BRASS

$3\frac{1}{2}$

$2\frac{1}{4}$

$\frac{3}{8}$R

$\frac{3}{8}$R

CRUMB TRAY
$\frac{1}{16}$ ALUMINUM OR BRASS

3

6

BEVEL

$\frac{1}{4}$R

2

$\frac{5}{8}$R

BROOM HOLDER
$\frac{1}{8}$ ALUMINUM

2

$1\frac{1}{2}$

$\frac{1}{4}$R

$\frac{3}{16}$ D.- 2HOLES

$\frac{1}{2}$

$\frac{3}{4}$

$\frac{1}{8}$R.

$1\frac{1}{2}$

QUICKIE PROJECTS

SPUN RELISH DISH SET

1. Material: Bowls - aluminum, pewter or stainless
   steel (16 ga.).
   Base - walnut, cherry or rosewood.

2. Finish: Bowls - polished.
   Base - natural (oil finish).

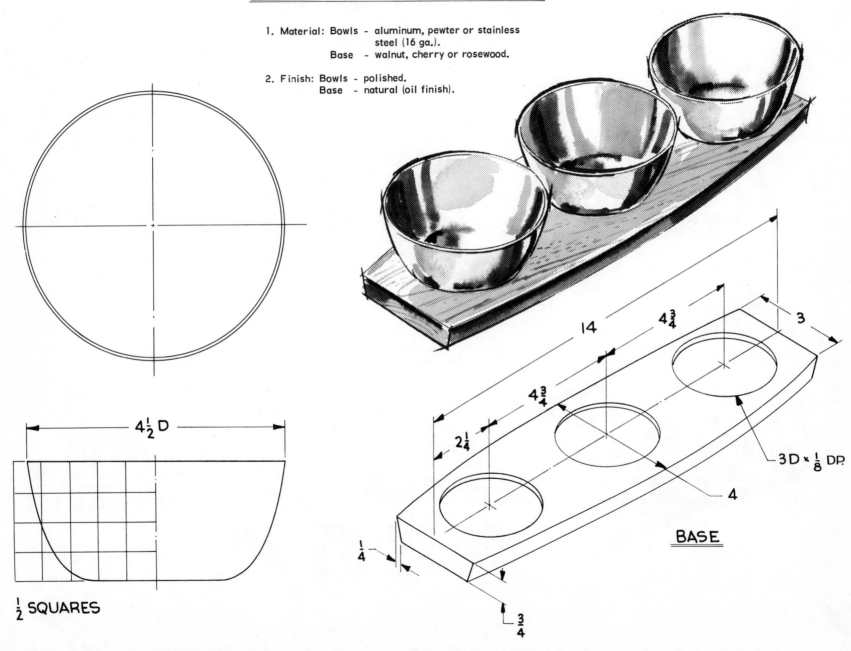

$4\frac{1}{2}$ D

$\frac{1}{2}$ SQUARES

14

$4\frac{3}{4}$

3

$4\frac{3}{4}$

$2\frac{1}{4}$

3D × $\frac{1}{8}$ DP.

4

$\frac{1}{4}$

$\frac{3}{4}$

BASE

LETTER

HOLDER

TYPICAL PERFORATED DESIGNS

1. Material: Perforated or embossed steel or aluminum sheet. 20 - 22 gauge.

2. Finish: Natural or painted flat black.

3. Remove all sharp edges.

4. Cement felt to feet to prevent scratching or marring surface of table or stand.

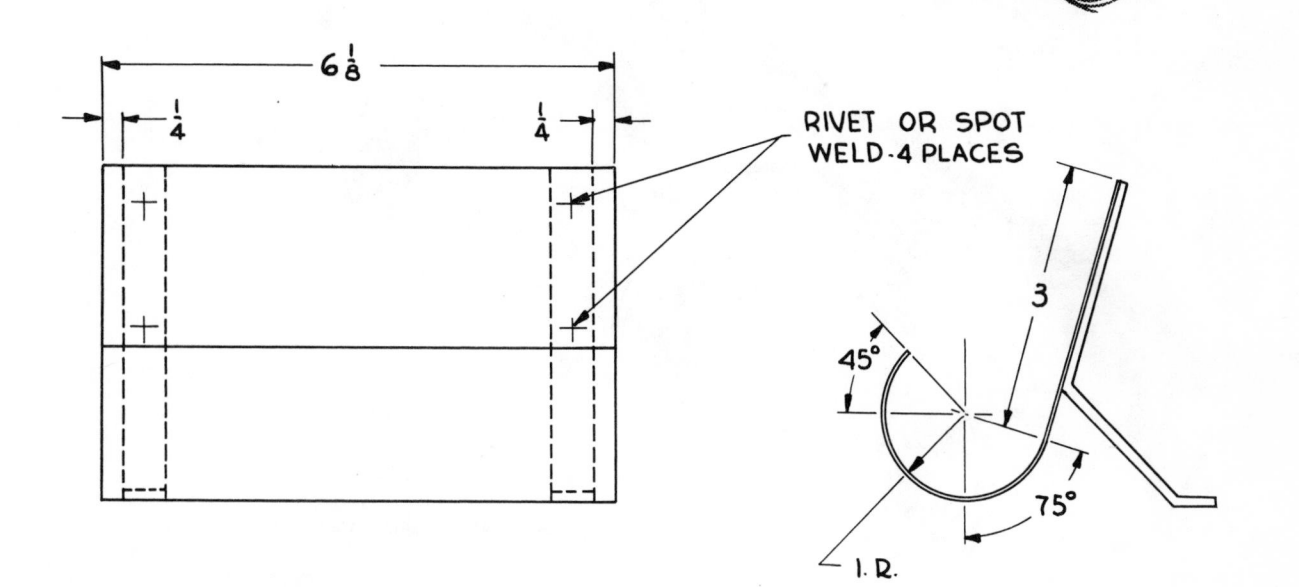

$\frac{1}{8} \times \frac{1}{2}$ STRIP

9 8 7 6 5 4 3 2 1

A B C D E F

$\frac{1}{2}$ SQUARES

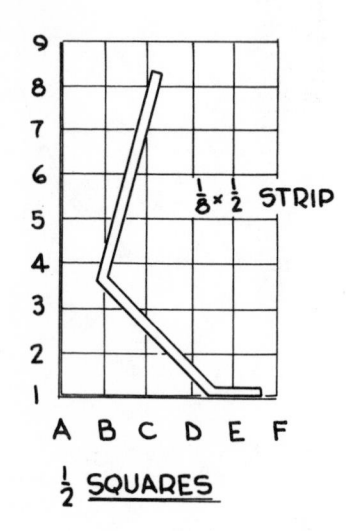

$6\frac{1}{8}$

$\frac{1}{4}$ $\frac{1}{4}$

RIVET OR SPOT WELD-4 PLACES

45°

3

75°

I. R.

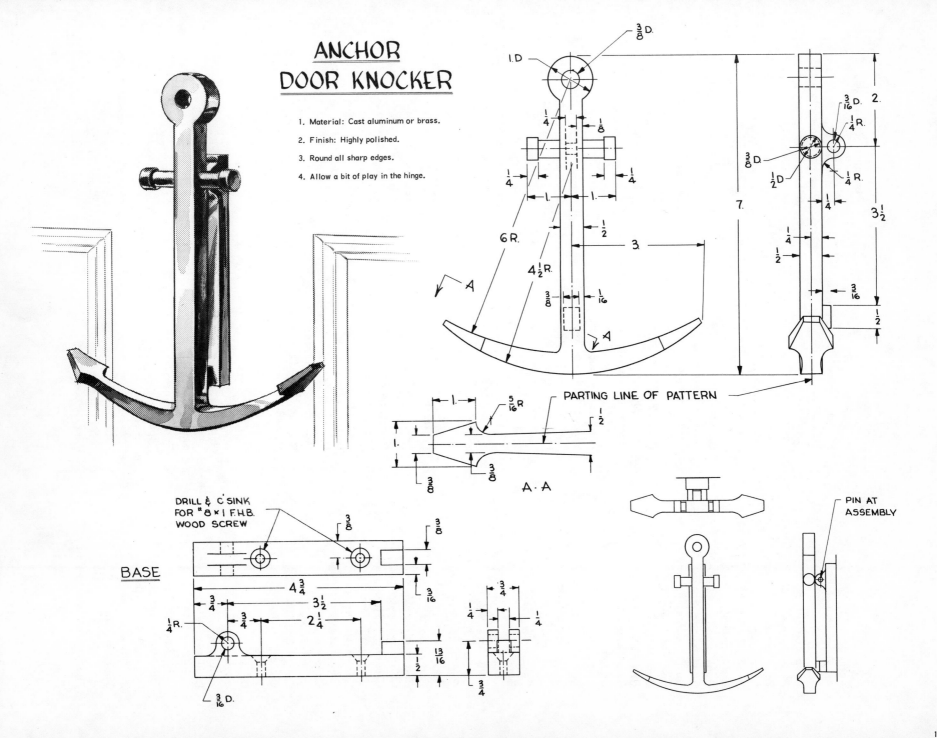

ANCHOR
DOOR KNOCKER

1. Material: Cast aluminum or brass.

2. Finish: Highly polished.

3. Round all sharp edges.

4. Allow a bit of play in the hinge.

PARTING LINE OF PATTERN

A·A

BASE

DRILL & C'SINK
FOR #8 × 1 F.H.B.
WOOD SCREW

PIN AT
ASSEMBLY

INDEX

112